This book was written over a few years in an attempt to reflect the authors view on human history and the potential future of our world.

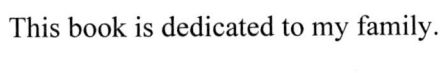

This book is dedicated to my family.

Richard A Stothert

ECHOES IN A VOID

A Human Future?

AUSTIN MACAULEY PUBLISHERS™

LONDON · CAMBRIDGE · NEW YORK · SHARJAH

A CIP catalogue record for this title is available from the British Library.

ISBN 9781035855681 (Paperback)
ISBN 9781035855698 (Hardback)
ISBN 9781035855704 (ePub e-book)

www.austinmacauley.com

First Published 2024
Austin Macauley Publishers Ltd®
1 Canada Square
Canary Wharf
London
E14 5AA

Table of Contents

Life

Life, intolerance, while time slips quickly by
The frosted glass of fate.
Sweet memories of incompatibility
Change to despair and shadowed death.

For what purpose do we live?
Knowing of eternal beauty and splendour
Waiting just around the corner.
To this there can be no answering.

One pattern, one path incomplete
Desiring, love, lust demolished! Returned to dust.
Now one and all to cry, repeat!

RAS 1966–1968

Author's Note

This document is a philosophical epistle written with no other thought than to record my views on the world of humans in the early twenty first century. In order to ensure current correctness, I will attempt to be politically correct throughout. I have referenced all human life irrespective of gender, religion, language or sexual orientation by encapsulating us all in the single word, Man. For clarity, I am not a scientist, politician nor a religious leader. Neither am I a behaviourist. I am simply an ordinary mature male bloke of the human species reflecting personal thoughts of and about Man.

This contains my view on our behaviours past and present and perhaps how the future may be for us all. My hope is that if what is written here encourages just one fellow Man to think differently about us and the planet we share, I will have achieved my intention. For ease of understanding, you will often find references to single Man, a tribe, or a clan or kin and even Man collective/s. I have not allowed myself to turn my thoughts into a fictional story but simply to reflect my view of potential options that we may face collectively going forward. I take full responsibility for any and all mistakes contained herein. If we of today are able to exorcise all fear of each other, create together a different Man society where each holds regard for the other and tolerance for our differences, perhaps there will be a long-term future for the great-grandchildren of our grandchildren.

This is written in hope for those whom we shall never meet.

What Is Man?

There is nothing in the world of today, or even tomorrow, that allows Man to stay on as part of this planet for very much longer. The fact that Man currently remains here as a species and has 'shared' this world for as long as we have is primarily due to our own imbecilic, weak attempts at controlling all that the planet contains. Man has an inbuilt chemical imperative which is the need to control or dominate all things, including other Man. Little matter the possible danger and destruction caused in doing so. Such control is, however, always just and only for our own tribe or kin, rarely for benefit to any Man collectives or for any geographically environmental benefit.

Control, including an incessant determination to prove that what I or my tribe, clan or Man collectives are, is, better at all things than any other Man. This is a basic life-state of all Man, from our simple cave-dwelling times where life was survival of the quickest, the fittest, the bravest, strongest or just the more cunning and agile. All these traits have dominated Man activities since our very early times here. All were and remain exclusively for the protection and comfort of Man against all others—animal, mineral, vegetable, crawling, flying, swimming, no legs to one hundred legs plus all living things in between. These ancestors of ours were, in reality, more than likely carrying out these activities not for any collective Man but rather for their immediate family, tribe or group members.

Often at the cost or detriment of other tribes or Man collectives or indeed any other species or 'issue' of Mother Nature.

Therefore, one can argue with ease that here we stand, thousands upon many thousands if not millions of years later and nothing has been absorbed by us to change or challenge this fundamental core of Man to Man behaviour. The strong will always dominate the weak and thus the strong will hold power. Well, at least until other Man arrives with a bigger stick, more money or greater knowledge.

Suffice it to suggest, however, that the modern 'caves' of Man, in some areas of the planet at least, offer more robust comforts today than those rock-holes utilised initially.

Sadly, to say though, very many Man still have not moved on from their caves either physically or metaphorically, even though the knowledge and technical capabilities are available to ensure that poverty and hunger of all Man can be eradicated. Social, political, religious and race conflicts across the world of Man staunchly ensures that continued poverty, hunger and degradation for millions of fellow Man remains. Such locations across the world of today simply reflect the essence then of the 'I am better than you' syndrome.

Perhaps today, Man has absorbed so much understanding of this world and his place on it that the perceived invincibility of some like-minded Man groups ensures that their reign of supremacy over and above all others, including all fellow issue of Mother Nature, is now and will forever remain.

Perhaps Not

Nothing can define in any clear or simple way the absolute stunning progress of this so-called 'animal' Man. The use of the word 'animal' here in its own way simply reflects the deep-seated conceit of Man to affix this title to itself and a collection of apparently similar living species. For thousands of years, Man has managed to learn from the natural things on this planet, to absorb these findings and their impact, retaining the gains then passing such knowledge onwards to surviving kin. These kin in their turn have expanded this rich inheritance often for the same basic deployment principles. For themselves. For the survival of their tribe, kin or group.

Sometimes, however, when the next additional piece of knowledge or understanding was discovered it may have created a pause, a sudden ponderous examination of its potential worth. The finder, or collective finders, may have been deeply shocked, concerned even, that the application of this new discovered learning might result in danger so it was considered expedient to keep such knowledge to oneself.

That some 'knowledge' has always been held 'secret' has been another stupidly common human behavioural rule since very early Man days, an activity undertaken irrespective of the potential for any inherent dangers.

This new piece of knowledge then was perhaps recognised to have *value* to the holder in a personal beneficial way for gain, protection or imagined superior power. Such actions of either a single Man or a single collective group of Man are a constant behaviour trait. 'Something' known was uniquely withheld from all other tribe members, or even any 'like-thinking' tribes or groups irrespective of any agreed apparent symbiotic relationship that may have existed between them at the time of discovery.

We know that Man migrated across our planet over time, constantly exploring, continuously seeking knowledge and understanding of our environment. Settling where there were plentiful supplies of natural foods, warmth, shelter and water. Such Man groups would eventually move on when these essentials were fully utilised either by over-usage or attacks of pestilence or indeed when chased away by other hostile Man groups.

Nevertheless, such changes of location provided learning about our world all the time. For example, that seasons existed and each came with its unique threats and opportunities. Over time Man learned to overcome the threats and to make use of the opportunities. Alongside seeking security for immediate kin, Man continually attempted, via cunning and stealth, to dominate all known wild beasts. Often such domination included the mass slaughter of non-human living creatures and, of course, 'other' Man groups. Sometimes, though, this activity was simply to expand their own Man tribe's location or influence. It is also well known that Man did indeed call upon other groups, semi-kindred or friends perhaps, to help face possible challenges collectively, thus providing a common understanding for self-protection or shared gain.

In such times of living jointly or in harmony with like-minded groups, each would sustain for the other an often-unspoken defence pact from other Man groups. These others, perhaps, were not of a like-mind or similar disposition. Maybe these 'others' were perceived to be somehow different in cunning, sharing, taking or giving. The result of such collaboration over the millennia has been the formation by similar thinking societies agreeing a 'like-with-like' association. These, of course, would and did change when 'like' tribes or groups became temporary enemies.

The results of all these associations, subversive or offering close partnership for mutual gain, continued throughout the aeons and are easily visible in the East-VS-West and other similar fractured areas of Man civilisation in the world of the 21st century. The principal cementing factors of such associations have always been many and vastly varied.

However, where they do exist, such relationship is due to the simple recognition that 'like-with-like' may provide greater strengths in moments of perceived or real collective adversity. Such relationships can also result in long-term cultural integration and mutual support. This has always been how the Man animal has behaved. No doubt this relationship behaviour will continue into whatever future there will be for us on this planet or even off it.

Matters of Division

Man then, often with like-minded groups, divided across the world creating over time creed, race and ownership of settled locations. Each Man collection built their own community behaviour, structure, social rules and languages, only to be challenged or threatened by other Man collectives including non-Man threats such as wild beasts. However, 'Mother Nature' acting as a provider of so much good also provides for and takes steps to disallow domination, or potential domination, by any single issue of hers by any other of her 'issue', on this planet.

Nevertheless, and perhaps as a result of potential dominance, many of the species of an enormously wide variety on the planet have disappeared across the aeons. Where dominance by one species becomes an inescapable outcome and threatens potential destruction, Mother Nature will step in to take charge, applying whatever remedy is needed to dispose of the offending offspring. Perhaps the same fate is not now too far away for Man?

Where Man was to be the recipient of such action in the past the application of those microscopic dangers invisible to Man, deadly germs, have frequently provided the desired result. These two opposing life forms often used throughout the history of all life on this planet have always resulted in the partial annihilation of each other at times of application.

An action taken as a species control mechanism by Mother Nature or as a mass-culling process of any of her issue, including Man, has been applied when required throughout the history of this world. Nevertheless, the smarter Man became over time the more able he has become to protect himself against such natural population control methods. As a direct result of this gained knowledge, shared or not, Man himself has developed his own Man capability for the application of mass-culling population control. Not just for any perceived natural threat to its own existence but of even greater diabolical stupidity, to use against its fellow Man.

Yes, Man uses its own knowledge as a mass-culling capability against itself.

Throughout Man's history, it is known that such developed knowledge has been used exclusively for the benefit of a single tribe, or individual. Just one example is Genghis Khan. With his growing army made up of masses of Man bludgeoned into loyalty to him, he slaughtered without too much hesitation many millions of Man. The actual total remains unknown but current estimates suggests this to be in excess of 11 million people at the time. This in his drive across large swathes of Eurasia to establish a 'safe' and *acquiescent population* for the foundation of his own empire.

In other words, his was an army built on fear of death by a despot who considered himself the living master of all Man. It is, however, regarded today, from an academic point of view at least, that this mass-culling of Man by Man at the time may have been beneficial in securing life resources for all humans by reducing what was thought to be an over population of Man in the 'known' world at that time.

Genghis Khan, though, is just one such example of so very, very many where Man will dominate or slaughter other Man in a stupidly biased attempt to prove a false 'specialness'.

How much of humanity was slaughtered during the so-called 'Holy Wars' when the Lion Heart set out to save Jerusalem is actually unknown but estimates are very high.

Man's profane secular obsession with oneself being of a 'higher' order or the only 'correct' or righteous community often teaches its followers that all other Man are, by definition, wrong.

"They must, therefore, be made to agree our clan's cultural superior status or face force to do so," an attitude of human behaviour that still divides the Man populations of the world of today.

Yes, the stupidity of Man slaughter by Man continues.

The second world war of the twentieth century, a six-year conflict, is estimated to have seen the 'culling' of Man by Man of between 50 million to 80 million individuals. The higher total estimate includes millions who suffered death due to war-related disease and famine. There is a suggestion that such acts of this nature by Man may provide a respite for Mother Nature in her programme of issue culling and control. But the 'second world war' was only one such conflict in that century.

Estimates for the whole of that century, regarded as the bloodiest in recorded Man history, reach a staggering number in excess of one hundred and ninety million people who died in Man against Man conflicts across our world between the years 1900 and 1999. This equates to approximately 10% of the known Man population on this planet in 1913. About 1,900,000 Man slaughtered each year of the past century. War between Man collectives also provides opportunity, for those so inclined, to invest huge amounts of energy and money seeking the very next best fastest Man-killing innovations.

Matters of Man Division Indeed

Throughout the aeons, though, there can be no challenge against suggesting that Man has become the principal creature of earth-bound life on this world. Proving to be the only known creature of all land issue of Mother Nature able to absorb, share, question, learn from and pass on acquired knowledge to benefit or threaten future Man generations.

While most non-Man creatures are seen to repeat the behaviour of their ancestors' activities this seems mostly a simple auto-copying of such behaviour. Not a *learning* from, or of more importance, a *reasoning* of the behaviour itself. With the ability to 'think', and to discard irrelevant matters, Man' has gathered volumes of knowledge initially recorded in, or by, individual tribal behaviour or custom.

This has been handed down to generation after generation providing opportunity for continued learning and utilisation of such knowledge. The application of learning generally would be used by Man in his environment almost always exclusively for the benefit of a single tribe or group or Man collective. Once visual external character depiction capability was commonplace, albeit initially via painted rock (cave) wall or other 'shape' application (of which hieroglyphics on papyrus is just but one example) such written records may have *excluded* knowledge which was not regarded by members of the 'recording tribe' or an individual as of any importance or group benefit. Such pieces of knowledge then would not be given or passed on at all. They would potentially be 'lost' for ever or until perhaps rediscovered at another future point in time.

If the above can be regarded as to hold any truth at all, even just as a possibility, then it cannot be too difficult or unjustified to also suspect that matters considered to be of extra special or specific gain were to be withheld and kept *secret* irrespective of any consequences, good or bad. These would also have been excluded or prevented from being available for general consumption. Such matters would not be passed on to the family, tribe or group or collectives due perhaps to some perceived significant benefits of ownership to the holder or leaders.

This activity of 'hiding' knowledge away clearly reflects an explicit standard of *behaviour* of all established Man tribes throughout Man history, irrespective of race, creed, social environment, practices or political doctrine. Therefore, in the world of the 21st century where, by its own acknowledgement, Man faces possibly its greatest survival challenges caused mainly due to its own folly, the same base-root Man behaviour of not sharing some knowledge with other Man continues.

The folly continues even today.

This may be on the pretext that this recently gained or acquired knowledge is supposedly protective in some way. Even a new power, perhaps, leading to some form of mockery of other Man by public statement that 'We're better than you' or, 'We know something stronger than you' behaviour.

A new tool to deploy at will over all others, perhaps. Today, still, there are many State-held Knowledge Secrets of each and every modern Man tribe, or collective that are purposely withheld from view. If a particular tribe is under serious threat of imminent conquest, the so-called 'leaders will ensure destruction of such apparently unique knowledge. An action aimed at giving false support to the incumbent leaders' previous denials of the existence of such knowledge.

This behaviour then begs the question as to how much collective knowledge of all Man tribes has been lost deliberately to prevent others from benefiting by access to such knowledge throughout the millennia? This, of course, cannot possibly be quantified with any real level of accuracy.

However, it would be exceedingly foolish—which, of course, Man, irrespective of tribe or group, is known to be very skilled at being—to contemplate that such a basic tribal behaviour is not practiced today by all Man tribes. This is irrespective of loud public denial alongside statements of real and lasting 'friendship and support' of and for other tribes. Actively designed deceit by all Man to all Man relationships today continues to reign supreme in the 21st century world. A political, religious and society theatre of denials playing constantly to full houses in every corner of the planet.

So Here We Are in the 21st Century AD

That is unless, of course, some existing brethren of a particular following, creed, dogma, tribe or clan may not agree with such a statement due to a specific set of beliefs, morals or principles. Generally, however, Man has for the purpose of synchronisation in large parts of the globe agreed to adopt the Medieval Latin 'Anno Domini' (AD) (meaning 'in the year of the Lord' but now amended to 'In the Year of Our Lord') to be the recognised moment, a single 'point in time', as an established benchmark for the modern global recording of the passage of time This is recognised even by specific Man tribes today that hold within their own faith or particular cultural foundation an alternate passing of time or ages. Nevertheless, the current accepted 'norm' is as depicted in the AD status above measuring the passage of time both before and after the agreed benchmark.

Many Man groups do have other thoughts but allow for such a methodology to be deployed in the interest of world collective recognition for the purposes aforesaid.

Such an agreement or joint understanding of time passing in years, months, days, and hours down to seconds is a

remarkable achievement of all collective Man on this planet.
Sadly, though just one such common assent of so very, very
few.

There is no real recognition why the English words
'Before Christ' (BC) have been used alongside the Medieval
Latin words of Anno Domini. Suffice it to say that this may
simply be a reflection of the possible global influence of the
English language over the last thousand years or so. In line
with the current political-correctness of non-offending, the
term CE (Common Era), is today increasingly used to avoid
any specific religious connotation.

Currently, the world living population of Man is
approximately 7.4 billion individuals. This is expected to
climb to 9.7 Billion by the year 2050 increasing to 11 Billion
by year one of the 22nd century. This is a staggering expected
growth rate of just under 49 percent of the current Man
population worldwide in around 80 years! There can be no
more challenge to the continued existence of Man on this
planet than that expected growth rate of the human race. This
population growth will not fall within those areas of the world
often referred to as the 'Developed World' of today. Of
course, populations in these areas will indeed grow but at a
slow and possibly national absorbent capability rate. The
major growth expected areas are those in areas such as Asia
and Africa. These are in the 'under developed' areas of the
world already struggling in some cases to maintain viable
feeding, infrastructure and education policies at local level.

How much withheld (secret) knowledge from the
beginning of the time of Man may have helped to provide
answers to some or even all of the current natural resource and

environmental challenges of our time, we shall never know. How far Man is along the path of self-annihilation cannot be truly estimated. Man continues, however, to push, some say rush, towards its own extinction and there is little argument to slow the pace or work together as one to ensure any future for all Man.

It is clear, however, to many individuals in the community of Man that the journey to self-annihilation is well beyond halfway and gathers exponential momentum daily.

As an issue of Mother Nature, Man today is a plague, a pestilence even, which appears to be devouring at a substantially alarming rate all that it and millions of other life forms depend on to survive. This is what Man has become due to and by its own, now almost fatal, conceit. Tribe attacking tribe to gain what? 'Like-with-Like' strutting and puffing to protest their innocence of any part of historical human abhorrence's. Thus, our tribe, clan or collective alone are the righteous and will inherit the Earth above and beyond all others because ours is the only true and 'correct' Man society.

Perhaps only theirs is the 'light' leading to Man's ultimate salvation.

Perhaps not!

Hover a Moment (Who Are We)

This has to change: this tit-for-tat, the shouting, the pouting, the lying, with all the pushing back! Mankind is over without a single thought that tomorrow brings nothing at all, just naught. The learning and processes that history has wrought shows that, banish the thought, we are but nothing as the world travels forth. Not a single blade of grass have we made nor saved nor the forests for decades after decade! The air we breathe, now sodden with man's sheer mess, kills us and all that we profess to be the best or hold dear. What then to do that has to be done as mankind's future shall surely soon be bygone!

Without our footprint, this world will, of course, repair to sail fair across the millennium yet to be in its rightful place throughout eternity. With current Man remaining upon its shore though the world cannot see the full future long. The poison we have brought has blinded the way so how on earth could it be possible for us to stay? We kill the atmosphere, the water the grass alongside each and every bomb that we blast across this world, destroying any safe path ahead.

Hover a moment! Won't you just stop! Look, see, hear the weeping of those not free. The crying of the already dead and the dying of all that nature brings. No remorse for us who are now of course the common vermin stock which Mother Nature is sure to stop. The creatures, the plants supporting all life are dying as a result of our constant strife. So, let's stand together, if you have the nerve, before Mother Nature provides in its entirety all we deserve. But will we hold hands across the seas exploring our willingness to reflect?

Surely there can still be a remedy, a way of sharing yet between all that is humanity. Forget the kinships unique as they stand let's for once play a collective hand in attempting to find a better play. There can be no truth no trust in all that we say without first scrubbing away the corrupted behaviour of Man. To the language of nature all-natural things adhere, keeping Nature's rules to survive and prosper. Yet we fail, we toil without foil to comprehend that there is an end to us all.

Take a single word or two from the above examine their realities seeking out the Dove that will bind us all together. Thus, can be achieved once we really believe, a way for us to stay. Human life. No matter the language spoken, grunted, sung, clicked or snorted or written or reported it is always rife with less than forsooth! 'TRUTH' then shall we start with on this pondering itch before all humans are reduced, rendered to nothing, sent forever off the pitch.

Truth then is dealing in fact, not altered or amended, plotted or twisted, nor spat to reflect one's own murky twisted shade. 'FACT' is real, actual, to see, perhaps to touch, a genuine reality. Not yours or mine to bend or hide or exploit or corrupt to full ambiguity. Fact is where we can

all hold fast, composed, conducted ready to grasp and pull
full force to build a future true.

Without holding hands corruption will continue anew.
Forlorn! Leaving no future nor way forward for me…or for
you…or those not yet born.

Hover a moment! Won't you just stop!
Look, see!
Hear the weeping of those not free!

RAS (November 2016)

Oh Stupid, Stupid Man!

With a real openness of vision, it becomes very clear that
even in light of all the knowledge gathered by Man over
thousands of years, the application of that knowledge via
utilisation of technology is, in reality, a testament to the
absolute stupidity of Man. Nothing, but nothing in our
amplitude has been gained since our cave-dwelling, crawling,
early days that will save our future! It is today simple for Man
to categorise each Man by setting a benchmark 'test' to
establish the Intelligent Quotient (IQ) of another, others or all.
But such 'tests' drawn up by some apparent academic
brilliances do it without acknowledging a basic simple fact.
Some of those so tested may utilise a greater intellect power
than those who set these tests. Such individuals are able to
deploy that very ability to escape awareness of it by
manipulation of the tests designed to measure such capability!

When will this ever be accepted and recognised?

Do these members of this Man species perhaps offer a real
chance of building a collective long-term survival plan? We

can send craft to the other side of our universe. But still we throw away tonnes of plastics under hedgerows and bury nuclear waste in the oceans daily across our world knowing the danger that such Man-made material holds for the future. We have a space station circling our planet *(another common assent-venture by Man between a small but powerful group of Man collectives)* with Man aboard, yet we constantly poison our atmosphere each and every hour of every day.

We have made exceptional strides in medical sciences for the prime benefit of Man, yet we spend billions to trillions of cash each year building weapons to kill each other en-masse. A single Man today can communicate by live video link with any other individual or gathering of individuals (tribe, clan, kin, even enemy) located anywhere on this planet or even off it, all in real time.

Yet millions of Man face war, poverty, depredation, starvation, abuse and death needlessly, day after day, most of which is driven by the greed and callousness of other Man. There is always 'profit' in war and the constant plight of others.

Well-intentioned individuals or organisations of concerned Man collectives will set out to provide basic survival necessities to such devastated groups. They are attempting the seemingly impossible of the clear and precise purpose to provide succour in whatever form is needed to achieve their objective. However, backroom 'deals' must be done in the shadows by the festering combatants lords and governors. Money and/or weapons are exchanged alongside deals to share the ultimate spoils of the current conflict. All this is accompanied by outright bribes made in order for the solace-offering-parties to fulfil their goal. These possible providers of care are often deliberately killed by either side of the argument or conflict. This is simply to prove that 'they can be killed' on the orders of the senior leaders any time even when they have agreed not to do so.

A wrangle that may last for days, weeks, sometimes months, while the suffering recipients wait to die from lack of access to water, food or medicines. Despotic so-called 'leaders' of Man tribes, clans, etc., steal from and kill their own kin at will to sustain their glorious, apparently God-given, lifestyles with not a care for any compassionate voiced members of their community. These bigots, however, always reach out with their begging-bowl-hands across the world of Man, seemingly pleading for help for their own tribe.

But rest assured that any such donations given simply will not get to their starving or sick tribe members. Such grants are known by the sponsors to line the pockets of the 'leader or leaders' in such countries or communities. Nevertheless, each sponsor retains a pious clear moral conscience and stance of public purity. So false pious Man gives to show generosity to all other Man groups, always knowing the sickly, sardonic mocking laugh of the recipient echoes in his own private wealth-filled cave.

Man Is Lies and Secrets

It is easy to understand the essence of this core Man behaviour. It has been within us from the very beginning. Using the modern idiom, "it is as much in our DNA as breathing." A piece of each Man deep within and just as necessary as the physical presence of a heart and lungs, is an inbuilt dominance demanding self-preservation.

This requires blatant deceit and secrets in equal measure, no matter what these two behaviours will entail. Man has not evolved to become a master of universal social deceit, Man simply is and throughout history has proven to be born, the master of social deceit. Not a learned activity, but a congenital truth. Even those creeds with very large numbers of followers offering a 'hope' possibly or even a reason for the very existence of each follower together with promises of a future life, are just as deceitful. They think that they are somehow special or selected so that they *alone* shall inherit the earth. This same collective will repudiate the claim of any other collective Man creeds declaring that their particular 'truth' is the only real one.

History reflects how such Man creed, groups, are constantly the purveyor, the driver of mass Man destruction. Mother Nature, therefore, in intimate crafty awareness of her issue and its hard-coded behaviour, has, in creating Man, ensured a non-reversible self-destruct 'gene' which is immersed in each Man, to protect her fully. This has so often proven to be a faithful servant. There is, to some degree, an almost poetic dark art to dialogue used displaying this level of Man contempt. An inexhaustible contempt not only for all other Man but also towards Mother Nature herself. For example, the ability that Man has, without even a pause or hesitation, to address or verbalise in public a statement on a particular stance while actually believing the opposite. Thus, hiding his own belief on the matter addressed. Answering direct questions via a collection of incomprehensible collective words that are simply sounds providing a shield of noise to avoid a direct answer. These uttered sounds will contain no 'truth' on the subject matter.

They smile with outstretched hands knowing that such action hides contempt or despising for the recipient, hoping that they will believe your lies, but clearly knowing that they will not. In the same way, the recipient will smile and shake hands knowing that their own words of reply in their answers given will not reflect their true belief. Examples of this Man behaviour flow in their multitudes across daily interactions on an ever-expanding constellation of matters both new and long standing. This behaviour is not just confined to those who adorn a 'political' persona or front. The same trait is reflected in, across and between many Man interactions.

Propaganda and Fact

Proving the unlikely marriage of the above two words is so very, very easy. Today it is accepted and even perhaps common knowledge across the so-called educated populations of the world that around fifty percent or more of all that Man believes at any single point in time to be true and factual will in FACT be proven not to be true at some time in the future. Knowing such a state of affairs exists and electing to accept that this statement is itself a FACT can, however, to a large degree be accepted as a true statement in the year 2020.

FACTs or knowledge of such 'truths', therefore, will play quite a large part in general terms in guiding the behaviour of all Man tribes, clans, groups. Assuming society's activities and behaviour are based on a collection of factual knowledge of which over half will prove to be untrue, the foundation for such Man behaviours of today may at any point in the future, be dispelled. This being a true statement then something, a mechanism of vagueness or an opaque reflection of a 'stated fact' has to be in place to fill a potential 'black-hole'—a future protector. A leader or collective leadership will, for example, all foster the use of misinformation (the opaque un-reality) across their statements. This may act as 'the' alternate reality to only be used should the future prove the current specific statement of facts to be false. These smart leaders of the tribes/masses/followers must then employ some way of filling that 'Truth' void or potentially face serious challenges to their own credibility when perhaps an espoused 'fact' of yesterday or yesteryear is later proven to be false.

Covering-up of the truth by officials or the collective elite must not be exposed, as fact though, it can be and can represent a potentially serious threat to own clan, tribe, collective, safety. What is used to secure that any former protestation or avowal accredited to such Man leader or collectives, or officials, was sincere at the date and time of its utterance? Supporting PROPAGANDA of course!

Used if only to cover the possibility that such statement is later proven wrong! Hence, the art of defensive or protective PROPAGANDA is born.

There are so very many examples of such Man leaders escape strategies throughout recorded time where PROPAGANDA has been the constant although, perhaps, the strangest of bedfellows of spoken or recorded FACTs across much of Man history.

Just one such small example is a 'FACT' held to be true for over two hundred years, initially to protect the pronouncement by an apparent learned medical man of high standing and this Man's associates.

Tomatoes!

Although grown in southern Europe for many years previously, it was not until the late 1590s AD that they were introduced in England and began to be grown. These fruits, originally from South America were, however, regarded by the medical science and learning of the day to be unfit for human consumption, even potentially poisonous, and therefore declared to be dangerous! This, even though it was known by these same learned people that tomatoes were eaten by humans in Spain and Italy at the time and of course throughout South America. Nevertheless, for over two hundred years across British colonial influences, including North America, they were regarded as 'interesting inedible plants with bright red fruit'.

It was not until early in the 19th century that they were proven to be of little or no harm at all. In FACT, in the first half of the 19th century the humble tomato rapidly entered the vegetable and salad diet of the English population even though it was subject to continued discussion about being, in some areas of science, classified strictly as a fruit.

Those who held the high posts of learning in England throughout the 17th and 18th centuries maintained the espoused and recorded 'FACT' of the established medical knowledge, that tomatoes were possibly poisonous and dangerous. What these individuals could not abide, of course, was having to acknowledge to the world at large that any single member of their educated elite held in high regard, could possibly have been mistaken.

Propaganda, lies and whitewash maintained the esteem of both the individual and the group for over two hundred years until reality…that of mass Man tomato consumption exploded the long-held myth.

So many such examples exist where fact and propaganda share centre stage of Man behaviour, each harvesting the benefit of the other just in case the one is to be 'found out'. I use the tomato story here for its obvious level of contempt held by the elite for, of and against the common Man in the United Kingdom and colonies.

Finally on this matter and sadly using that same medical science community, when the 'horseless carriage', was clearly about to take over from the real horse pulling power, it was avowed by all 'experts' medical and humanitarian in the United Kingdom, that the human body would disintegrate should it ever reach a speed greater than twenty-five miles per hour. Hmmm! Oh fact-vs-propaganda-vs-reality.

Love Vs Hate

Much has been written by thousands upon thousands of Man individuals, collectives, academics or just a single Man for thousands of years all driven by the emotion called in English, love. Millions upon countless millions of words in all languages talk of love. Many millions of songs have also been written as have poems, specific music and prose all dedicated to the feeling of and about love. Yet where are the equivalent or comparable volumes of words about hate? After all, massive amounts have been written about War and Peace, so where are all the words about hate?

Man, in all societies of any century seeks desperately to find that 'love' for, of and by another which is true and lasting. It is regarded as the principal positive key to fulfilling a real basic human need. That of a unique bond with another so strong that it will endure all the traumas, all the distraction that living may throw at the couple on their life-long shared journey. Is it real? Does it even exist? Can 'love' be taught? Why is it lost or broken or too often never, ever found? Adult Man generally will 'love' without fear of contradiction any issue that are born or adopted into such a strong human relationship.

Sadly, there are many other Man 'issue' who, not being from such a strong bond as mentioned, may not receive that level of adoration.

But the term 'love' is also claimed for the likes or dislikes of individual or collective Man. This different love covers millions of areas of Man behaviour. A life-long supporter of a sport, for example, will often state that they 'love' this sport. Some 'love' art of any description, still others 'love' mountains in springtime, yet more 'love' snow, or the sun or the sea, even all wild creatures; the list is endless!

Nearly all Man still recognise, however, the intrinsic essence of a long-term one-to-one 'love' relationship between two people. This recognition, this deeply quiet respect of such 'love' holds true throughout huge numbers of modern Man. Nevertheless, there are those communities of Man who may see such a relationship as the work of the devil (if such a being or 'thing' actually exists) or worse still, as an affront to themselves and their creed, society or beliefs, a defiance of their own life 'order'.

Such negative reaction to 'love' between others in these circumstances may prove catastrophic for any adult Man experiencing this strong shared 'love' with another in such societies. 'Love' itself may also be for a belief in something nebulous such as a religion, a collective conviction of a life hereafter.

Again, millions of words on such a belief across the millennia have been written. Some Man collectives such as religions, for example, have created unique activities that reflect their belief with songs and music that have been handed down for generations. This may include such things as chants, mantras, hymns and so on. All of these will reflect a passion, a love for the belief and its fundamental hope and teachings. Such teachings may give rise, however, to a passionate devotee of a particular belief or sect believing that theirs must be the only true way to an afterlife. They can be driven by blind passion to include all of Man in their collective belief.

Those that may deny this particular belief by following other views or doctrines will not therefore agree and are seen as an insult, an affront, they are 'unclean'. This defying of such a perceived reality may prove very dangerous to any third party. This is a Man behaviour locked into his DNA that has existed in many tribes, groups and collectives throughout history and has so often been directly responsible for Man against Man slaughter over millennia past and may potentially continue into millennia yet to be.

So where are all the written words about HATE?

Check with most modern languages and the antonym of the word 'love' or its equivalent is the word hate. Where are the musical compositions celebrating hate? The poems, sonnets, plays and prose. It is clearly accepted that the emotive response to physical attraction by Man to another has throughout history been proven to exist and called 'love' and is part of the DNA of every Man. Is this opposite emotion also a part of human DNA? Is each Man born with these two conflicting emotional attributes or capabilities? Can they cancel each other out? Is Man as much born to love as to hate? If so, can we individually, or better still perhaps by mutual endeavour, even collectively, learn to control either of these embedded Man traits? Or should we even try?

While 'love' may be regarded as intrinsic to Man, hate cannot be fundamental; it is *taught, learned* or *implanted* by external influences ...mainly other Man.

When opposing soldiers, each with gun in hand, suddenly face each other, will they each attempt to kill the other because of hate? In other words, can 'hate' be *manufactured* or induced through circumstance or obedience to order? If so, then both will be reacting to a kin, tribe or group-imposed demand or expectation potentially driven by propaganda. In such a case, it would be safe to assume that hate has indeed been synthesised. Perhaps the drive by each is to acquire some prize on behalf of their tribe, or collective tribes, a trinket for fulfilling an often false but championed cause? Or could it be simply the oft-chanted mantra in such instances of to *kill or be killed*?

If the latter is true, then surely and inherently without pause or thought, the self-preservation instinct becomes the absolute automatic individual Man response master, not hate. This means the reaction is a totally uncontrollable instinctive action that an individual Man cannot control. This is a mind-state existing for a just micro-second in time. It cannot be hating, but a base-linked survival mechanism.

Accepting that 'Love' cannot be manufactured by Man, how can hate be the opposite of Love if it is driven by circumstances of loyalty to a particular tribe, kin, group or creed? Jealousy can also manifest itself into hate as indeed propaganda and lies will corrupt emotions collectively or individually into hate. So, is 'to hate' an indoctrination of an easy mind, even whole nations? If indeed hate can be manufactured, such process requires an action by external influencers or a collective driven by third parties, perhaps, for personal or collective gain.

Maybe, then, a perceived (manufactured) negative circumstance attributed to or by another Man or thing can result in a single Man or collectively multitudes of Man reacting with an encouraged hate. As stated, Man provides its own self-culling process, very often by contrived suggestion via the use of propaganda leading to mass encouraged hate. This Hate will be driven through allegiances of communities subjected to indoctrination within a creed, kin or like-minded Man group at a time.

This 'encouragement' of the populace to a specific hate will be deployed if a challenge, real or imagined, is expected. Finally, convicted to this cause then, real Man to Man Love *cannot* be manufactured. So, for the purpose of this entreaty I submit that, Love will not result in Man mass-culling of Man. But hate, infused by propaganda and institutional lies or religious furore, can result in the manufacture of hate and could result in the mass killing of Man by Man.

Often, such slaughter has been driven via intolerance of other Man or driven by jealously. The base instinct controlling the mass application of hate must therefore be self-survival and protection of 'own'. Controlling or directing the mass application of hate must be by subjection of one tribe, creed or collective to propaganda from its leaders creating a false belief of injustice towards them by another tribe, creed or collective.

It is time now for Man to develop a new approach to securing a long-term future for all Man recognising difference with tolerance irrespective of race, creed, religion, language?

OR IS SUCH A THOUGHT SIMPLY A STEP TOO FAR FOR MAN?

In 1945, fifty countries from around the world met in San Francisco in an attempt to draw up an international charter based on submissions and proposals from China, the Soviet Union, the United Kingdom and the United States. The objective was to secure a future of international peace and prosperity via a collective intent to seek an end to the devastation and cruelty of war so that such conflict could never happen again.

In June 1945, the representatives of some fifty countries signed the Charter and on the 24th of October in the same year, the United Nations charter was ratified by China, France, the Soviet Union, the United Kingdom and the United States of America with all the original fifty signatory countries, plus Poland. Thus, the United Nations officially came into being in 1945 to be the agreed vehicle to a secure platform for all nations to discuss, with respect and determination, differences and disagreements with the simple task of resolving issues through discussion, and where possible, via compromise. This process had the primary aim that war would never again be the inevitable outcome of differences between nations across this world, and be an opportunity to gain peaceful resolution for all Man.

In the year 2018 AD (CE), there are 195 countries in the world, of which, 193 are UN members and 2 held 'observer state'. The following is copied directly from the UN website 71 years later, on Armistice Sunday!

Chapter 1 Purposes and Principles—Article 1. The purposes of the United Nations are:

To maintain international peace and security, and to that end; to take effective collective measures for the prevention and removal of threats to the peace, and for the suppression of acts of aggression or other breaches of the peace and to bring about by peaceful means, and in conformity with the principles of justice and international law, adjustment or settlement of international disputes or situations which might lead to a breach of the peace.

To develop friendly relations among nations based on respect for the principle of equal rights and self-determination of peoples, and to take appropriate to measures to strengthen universal peace.

To achieve international cooperation in solving international problems of and economic, social, cultural, or humanitarian character, and in promoting and encouraging respect for human rights and for fundamental freedoms for all without distinction as to race, sex, language, or religion and;

To be the centre for harmonising the actions of nations to attainment of these common ends.

Article 2. The organisation and its members, in pursuit of the Purposes stated in Article 1, shall act in accordance with the following Principles.

The organisation is based on the principle of the sovereign equality of all its members.

All members, in order to ensure to all of them the rights and benefits resulting from membership, shall fulfil in good faith the obligations assumed by them in accordance with the present Charter.

All members shall settle their international disputes by peaceful means in such a manner that international peace and security, and justice are not endangered.

All members shall refrain in their international relations from the threat or use of force against the territorial integrity or political independence of any state, or in any other manner inconsistent with the Purposes of the United Nations.

All Members shall give the United Nations every assistance in any action it takes in accordance with the present Charter, and shall refrain from giving assistance to any state against which the United Nations is taking preventive or enforcement action.

The Organisation shall ensure that states which are not Members of the United Nations act in accordance with these principles so far as may be necessary for the maintenance of international peace and security.

Nothing contained in the present Charter shall authorise the United Nations to intervene in matters which are essentially within the domestic jurisdiction of any state or shall require the Members to submit such matters to settlement under the present Charter; but this principle shall not prejudice the application of enforcement measures under Chapter V11.

***

In typical established Man behaviour, nothing, but nothing, has changed. There have been continuous Man conflicts throughout the past 70 plus years across this planet since the signing of the **UN** charter. The squabbles, disputes and invasions remain the unacceptable but *real* face of Man duplicity. While generally Man accepts and participates with each member providing senior representatives to work with and in accordance with the principles of the **UN,** confidence in this august assembly across the world is at best very low and at worst, non-existent. It is not too pessimistic to suggest that this 21st century may yet see the culling of Man by Man in far greater numbers than the last century.

The situation in and across the Middle-East and in particular the Syrian conflict, which is currently into its 9th year, continues unabated. The conflicting influences of the United States and Russia, where each are supporting different factions, may yet result in another global conflict.

Resolutions upon resolutions have been debated and issued by the UN yet they simply remain as 'bits-of-paper' ignored with open contempt by all parties. The continuous wars and sporadic violent situations following the rebirth of the State of Israel in 1948 AD continues to bemuse Man of the Twenty First Century. Again, the UN is incapable at delivering on the promises of member nations signed its charter. To me the UN just seems a place of well-meaning Bouncing Eunuchs.

The Bouncing Eunuchs!

I watched a war child die today, another slipped away beneath the smoking rubble.
While the Bouncing Eunuchs do nothing!
I watched a father cry today, his family, wife, mother and children all blown away.
While the Bouncing Eunuchs do nothing!
Washed up on the shore or boundary fence lie thousands of bodies of the innocent.
While the Bouncing Eunuchs do nothing!
Someone all in black and knife in hand severs a man's head for display, vile not grand
While the Bouncing Eunuchs do nothing!
The ones who sell bullets and guns, the cars, the bombs the uniforms are smiling well.
While the Bouncing Eunuchs do nothing!
The presidents, the leaders of this world, the kings or queens all talk in silent hope.
While the Bouncing Eunuchs do nothing!
We know what has to be done they cry as yet another year of slaughter goes by.
While the Bouncing Eunuchs do nothing!

The deceit of the corrupt in cunning despise, shake hands and smile while telling lies.
While the Bouncing Eunuchs do nothing!
Politicians all speak humbug and shallow truth, pointing at all others is their excuse.
While the Bouncing Eunuchs do nothing!
Those of religious fervour not involved in war simply stand and ponder…once more!
While the Bouncing Eunuchs do nothing!
Individuals trying to respond to cries for aid are held far too long until the bribe is paid.
While the Bouncing Eunuchs do nothing!
Barrel-bombs, poison gas and chemicals (germs) all banished of course, remain in full force.
While the Bouncing Eunuchs do nothing!
Who are these people representing Man' who cannot use the agreed solution plan?
While the Bouncing Eunuchs do nothing!
Lost is the dignity, the worth of a human person no equal rights in their dominion.
While the Bouncing Eunuchs do nothing!
Lost is justice respect for others opinion, rights to free and fair self-determination.
While the Bouncing Eunuchs do nothing!
Lost is the agreement to live in peace to practise tolerance with solace, offering relief.
While the Bouncing Eunuchs do nothing!

Homes destroyed, citizens lost displaced, as egotistic leaders attempt to save their face.
While the Bouncing Eunuchs do nothing!

Lost is love of human kind leaving nothing but cold self-interest behind, it's not me, see.
While the Bouncing Eunuchs do nothing!
Lost is international cooperation again, only misery death and despair continue to reign.
While the Bouncing Eunuchs do nothing!
So, they all hold polite discussion, even as a young dictator bigot develops mass destruction.
While the Bouncing Eunuchs do nothing!
How many more human clashes will it take, just to prove the UN charter is a FAKE?

RAS (February 2016)

Over nine years and as a direct result of something called in Man political spheres the 'Arab Spring' across the Middle-East region, a civil war has been raging in Syria. The following was written in 2013 when the search for chemical weapons held by the Syrian regime had concluded that the president did not have such weapons (proven later to be a lie by the use of these weapons on the people of Syria by their own government):

Syria…Oh Bloody future yet (crimes foretell the scale now due)
Chimes foretell the scale now due with counter-cries of fear and joy. From clangs via bangs with simultaneous task splintered with petit soft gentleness of germ. The fray that soaks us true but fails to break our practiced conceitedness!

49

Where is love among the dead, the broken and the dying, where is hope that thing of human fantasy. Lost in the money of the pockets that sponsor from afar claiming innocents but yet each has a future driven by blood and fostering of PRIDE to test their current and future method! Across the compass of all who hear and know the hand that love can supply hearing alone is not the only input sense forewarning of the combat due but Sight prevails burdened in constant enormity to penetrate awareness...so still they die!

It is due this week or next that conceited mongering of aligned dealers to take-up their bets on the blue or the red to be beaten again as the flag of death always wins while sponsors will seek to suggest and magically hype pity tears of shame from us prolonging patience...as their pockets fill.

While all good meaning sing and do nothing outside their pre-stated place to save the children, true they are the innocent yet to bend and break our sway because not this day will we have the might nor consider the need and push for all to read and fight that...Crimes foretell the scale now due.

RAS (on Syria, October 2013)
(The chemicals are found and removed; the not-involved can rest again; where is humanity?)

But the Brutal Civil
War Continues!

New Arrival (Syria, August 2016)

It arrived that morning from a cloudless sky, carrying a powder for me and you to die. Exploding just above the ground its arrival signal was nothing, just an explosive sound. No warning of the poison gas they had sent arriving to kill the children with no lament. So, we struggled to breathe choking on chlorine gas, eyes streaming, our lungs heaving. The children are never surprised, it is in their eyes, time now to die, without goodbyes.

Our president has sent this horrid gas trying to save his own, he is uncaring, he is crass. The world looks on without a real care as our young lives are taken, there is no despair. Just words floating between important states but each will protect their own pet hates. Our country is decimated, infrastructure devastated, no food, no water only pure hatred where has the love gone one to each other, where is life shared, brother with brother?

Some will survive twisted or broken but will one day shout for justice and be outspoken. Those of the East, the West, arguing or just watching this mayhem will never enjoy a rest until the truth is told the secret lies and deals shall be exposed for mankind to behold. No matter the unspoken depth of jealousy or hate, what they do now will be far too late!

Don't cry for Syria, killing is supported, allowed by East and West, but not fully reported. Our ancient culture is no longer required, now ruined, all holy sites gone, no sacred spires. The remnants cannot be repaired so will never be shared with the survivors of this land.

"This isn't war," our president has said, just supported terrorists there aren't too many dead!

East and West each disagree but so do the holy men, never may there be any harmony. So, sleep in peace all people in the world around, watch our demise, don't make a sound. Just address your souls, hearts and minds, reach out to your own God to stop the crimes. Goodbye from us, as most will soon be gone, to that life of quiet peace, beyond this one.

RAS (August 2016—Syrian government uses chlorine gas bombs on its own people)

And Continues!

New nursery rhyme—Syria Today
All speed up, all slow down the president's got a new master.

We shall duck, we shall dive the killing will now be much
faster!
Where's all the men who made the rules the Russians are
all full of laughter.

No one cares, no one's about to stop the Americans either.
The citizens die, there's gas in the sky the buildings are
falling much faster!
The cities are gone, destroyed for a song, all the bricks and
walls made of plaster.
The men of God, all chewing the cud are struggling to
provide a true answer.
So, we shall die, without a cry, but our country dies even
faster.
Oh…all…speed…up…oh…all…slow…dow….!

RAS (Weeping, September 2016)—read out loud to the
rhythm of 'See Saw Margery Daw'

And Continues!

ALEPPO (Syria, December 2016)

Any time now our long night will fall
Leaving a few to remain, if any at all.
Echoes abound in our shattered cave.
Pounding of guns destroy all we save.
Piercing blast hurt sad throbbing ears
Openly reminding us of the war years.

Sadness holds fast across all our land
Yet no one replies to our raised hands.
Revenge for defiance of strict control
Initiated by government takes its toll.
Agreed slaughter our President extols.

Decimation of citizens is completed,
East of Aleppo the fighters defeated.
Careful all the people allowed to flee
Empowered soldiers search for thee.
Members of the governing elite smile
Boasting they were right all the while.
Emergency status will remain in force
Russia will need to save face, of course!

RAS (Dec 2016)

Al-Assad, never elected by the Syrian people, continues their slaughter assisted by Russia while the rest of the world looks on. As in all Man conflicts since 1945, the 193 countries of the United Nations all display total impotence, while Russia has acted without fear of challenge.

Survival, Science,
Fact Vs Fiction

The clinging of, or attachment by, one very slightly negatively charged atom of oxygen to two very slightly positively charged atoms of hydrogen results in the creation of that essential to all 'life' on this planet, water (H_2O). This reliance on water by Man and many other life forms is of common knowledge to all tribes, groups and creeds across our planet. Here is an essential that has nothing to do with Love or Hate, Politics or Propaganda but to do with species survival. The science of the marriage of these different atoms may perhaps be less well known amongst the poorer populations of this world. However, all Man communities no matter where residing recognise the vital contribution water makes to life. Oxygen is, of course, produced in the air, in the ozone layer, as well as by algae and almost all bacteria, including aquatic plants that create oxygen during photosynthesis.

This merging of atoms resulting in such a vital contribution to all life on this planet is a scientific fact, not a piece of fiction. So much is the reliance of Man on water that in excess of 60 percent of the body weight of the average adult Man is composed of water. Again, a scientific fact, not fiction, is that oxygen is the largest natural element in Man. Without water then, all living things including the very existence of Mother Nature herself, will simply cease. This is not fiction or propaganda, nor is it a lie, it cannot be argued, politicised or shaped to suit a single tribe, kin, creed or group of Man collectives or even languages or religions. Without the creation of oxygen, there simply cannot be water.

Not the largest single providers on the planet of oxygen but a substantial contributor are green leaf trees. Some produce more than others depending on species or even location but all green trees manufacture oxygen. It has been stated by well-regarded scientific institutions that a mature green leaf tree is able to produce enough oxygen in one season to provide two mature humans enough air to breathe for a whole year. It has been estimated that one acre of green leaf trees is able to generate enough oxygen each season to support approximately 20 people for a year.

It is not fiction that as I write this today in September 2016 AD that some 9.5 million hectares (23.7 million acres) of deforestation by Man has taken place so far this year across the world. It is suggested by many that this level of tree destruction shows no sign of reducing at all. Only a very small number of replacements are ever planted to replace this loss of oxygen generation.

In addition to production of oxygen, all living trees inhale and store Carbon Dioxide (CO_2) a vital process for survival of living creatures on Earth. An acre of trees can absorb about as much CO_2 during a twelve-month period as that produced by an average size family car having travelled around 25,000 miles.

Without tree life on this planet the planet and all that Man has dreamed of for its future cannot happen. The single largest absorber of CO_2 on earth are plankton. Plankton consume an estimated 100 million tons of CO_2 every 24 hours. Dead trees make up a substantial portion of fossil fuel, the use of which over many centuries' past is today recognised as a major player in global warming. The latter has seen ocean water temperatures around the world increase by an estimated 2 degrees centigrade over the past many decades. Plankton numbers are reducing hugely as a result of this warming effect and thus their consumption of CO_2 is being seriously challenged. Unless reversed, the balance of nature supporting all life on this planet as we know it, is facing serious threat.

Even knowing this, Man continues to concoct false stories of self-integrity, pride in kin, tribe, group or creed. To keep secret 'bits' of knowledge to an individual, within a group or collective, to sustain continued learning on creating the 'best of the best' Man mass-culling potential while allowing millions to struggle in poverty and ignorance. Man, increasingly invests time, energy and money in creating their destructive capabilities much of which results in the depletion of the planets natural vital resources including water and tree resources each day. This truly reflects the level of the collective pig-headed conceitedness of Man. A behaviour that without change confirms the total mass imbecilic stupidity of all Man irrespective of kin, race, creed or location, collective associations, wealth, knowledge, or academic understanding.

How far has Man really progressed since our early existence where the essentials of survival were both bountiful, clean and unpolluted? Indeed, if Twenty First Century Man was able today to journey back to those times, how long would it take for the purity of the atmosphere at that time in history to kill this Man? Best guess? My best guess is less than five minutes. Such would be the clarity and purity of the air that together with adjusting to the natural vivid colours of the surroundings might demand a high degree of eye-protection. In fact, if such a journey was at all possible, the individual of today walking on the earth of past millennia would require to be in a hi-tech life-support protective suit. In other words, returning to the time of 'cave-dwelling' Man, the Man of today would be an alien on supposedly his home planet! Lacking his atmospheric mess of today would undoubtedly kill him. Time travel aside, the same would also apply to Man of the cave-dwelling era should by some time slip he suddenly found himself in the 21st century.

Time travel is fiction, so too is it to suppose that Man will continue to survive and prosper *without* changing its fundamental behaviour to all other Man and to Mother Nature. Agreeing to disagree but exploring together non-violent solutions to their differences of view while seeking understanding of and tolerance for others, holding hands working to secure a valid future for all. Is this really a step beyond this co called *intelligent* leader of all earth-bound species?

Regretfully, Man's future survival cannot be achieved on the basis of who has the most destructive mass Man-culling tools. Nor by control through fear and propaganda. Without a fundamental common behaviour change, the mass-culling by Man of itself through the application of military strength will be inevitable. If it is at all possible, any common behaviour change must not be tarnished by money or political doctrine as both are meaningless in such a determination for the future. Similarly, in a true attempt for long-term survival, all religions will have to prove tolerance and acceptance of all others. It cannot exclude any tribes, clans or groups of Man irrespective of secular status. All must have equal participation of the survival design process. It cannot be tarnished by money or political doctrine; both are meaningless in such a determination.

A global acceptance has to be achieved by the majority of Man that the future of this planet is now at very serious risk for all Mother Nature's issue. Building a positive and collective stance to deploy the best possible chance of success, is an action that must take precedence over all Man differences and endeavours. Without a basic change to our behaviour, standing together to save our collective future, it will not be too long until this planet will be rid of the current pestilence, Man. Once disposed of, Mother Nature will have the opportunity to repair and refresh her natural order of species and we can only hope prevent this planet from becoming yet another silent dusty world in the universe.

According to the CIA information on its open website, the published numbers for military spending by all nations across the world for the year 2015 was about US$1.8 trillion. Of which almost US$1 trillion was spent by just fifteen nations of the 195. These fifteen countries, just 7.7% of all the countries in the world, spent 50% of this total on their mass Man killing and defence capabilities. Some estimates reflect of a startling increase in spend by these same 15 nations as a percentage of global spending in the following year!

WHY?

Oh yes!

I know!

It is because they can!

Driven by constant propaganda, all governments and leaders of countries continue to maintain a constant fear-level in the populace that each is under threat from one or more of the others. It is, I think, fair to suggest that these same fifteen nations possibly have the largest communities of leading academics, scientists of every endeavour and generally well-educated populations. Clearly, they have strong economies and sophisticated societies. Can they all be so blind to their own corrupted, fabricated myths? Or are they just, as their history reflects, continuing to exploit the benefits of the bounty of their centuries of plundering, raping and pillaging across the globe? Can it be true, perhaps, to suggest that these current leading societies are trapped, metaphorically buried even, in their own historical mass propaganda? Therefore, are they actually nothing more than the proverbial hamster, running in its never changing circle, unable to escape its self-sealed fate, irrespective of knowledge or understanding gained?

The use today of mass Man culling weapons by any country in the world will simply accelerate the arrival of Man's final days on this planet. Such an acceleration will also see increased consumption of natural resources, increases in atmospheric pollution, all resulting in further poisoning and the rapid degradation of all oxygen producing and CO_2 absorbing living species.

Man *must* change his behaviour. Opportunity is available simply to undertake the actions determined in the United Nations charter to which all but two countries are signatories. In other words, to actually abide by the charter within the meaning and integrity they all are signed up to. If not, abandon the existing charter and collectively build one that provides certainty of a positive future outcome.

If Man is unable to change its behaviour in support of itself, indeed all the life inhabitants of this world, then recognition of this inability must include acceptance of defeat by all Man. Not one individual or nation or creed or religion, or culture. Defeat will be the collective responsibility. The pious, the lovers, those that breed hate, all the unspoken ones, all who don't care. Money and infamy, powerful and weak, there cannot be any survivors, as the result will be the *final* Man mass killing of Man.

Is this all that we are? Can we change?

Who am I?

I Am Today

I am born from darkness into the light
I am colours all of this world with sight
I am observing using un-focusing eyes
I am movement not being recognised

I am love and trust all rolled into one
I am vacant, really yearning to belong
I am life anew, an opportunity for you
I am tears of joy. Teach me what to do

I am laughter untainted, no corruption
I am sleep, no need for an interruption
I am happiness held close to give bliss
I am hope for a world near to an abyss

I am pupil learning to count and read
I am student seeing changes we need
I am adult now wishing to understand
I am politic talking via sleight-of-hand

I am cold, no cares for any yesteryear
I am music just out of tune, so unclear
I am reason, no acceptance of a myth
I am renegade not trusting herewith

I am old facing my final act of this play
I am corrupt, obstinate ashamed today
I am warrior unafraid of true deep pain
I am war killing others for some ill gain

I am human but no longer am I humane
I am intolerance any respect gone again
I am over, no more to leave, do or renew
I am past, no more can I say or do but...am I you?

RAS (October 2016)

Another Place Awaits?

A single Man's time here is short in the extreme. Humanity's time here should be endless.

Man is on a constant journey of learning and exploration and irrespective of any earth-bound status is fully conscious that each individual journey will end in death. Consequentially, procreation is essential. All people today and every day forward from today carry a responsibility to ensure that self-annihilation and destruction of this planet will not happen.

A change in behaviour is urgently required as a collective first step to the building of opportunity for a long-term future together. There has to be a recognition that all squabbles and concerns of historical or current circumstances are now irrelevant. History is gone. Let's build tomorrow's future today. Nothing of perceived reality in the world of existing Man continues forward. Not power or money, status nor ownership. Of greater importance, individual or collective greed, prejudice and violence must go. A new authenticity without reference to previous experience nor laden or encumbered with preconceived expectations awaits. A clean-sheet to work with.

Clear and precise meaning shall be reflected by all Man in reaching out to all others taking that first very brave and unique step into truth. Where 'hello' to a stranger is sincere with real peace. Where no one shall belittle any other nor cause abrasion between others. Tolerance shall answer fear with acceptance of differences and a true willingness to learn, to listen. Recognising that the best saving grace of Man will prove to be that of respect for, of, to and by each to the other. This planet is infinite in its gifts to its resident living creatures. Giving real knowledge and understanding of all life values, each to the other. Only this can offer a basic sound platform for a safe and secure future path for all Man to journey forward.

Shaping the future together today, building a common appreciation of all life and accepting that Man's past behaviours will have no place in tomorrow's future, requires a strong determination by all to succeed. Time for change, however, may be in short supply. Without doubt, the 21st century will deliver real threat alongside real opportunity. If we can grasp the opportunities by working together, the rewards will prove substantially beneficial to the future of all Man as we claim to so desperately seek irrespective of tribe, clan, race or religion.

When facing any serious turning point, having exhausted all other possibilities, there will always be just three potential actions.

The current really powerful nations, from a military perspective, face serious challenges in recognising that to dominate others through aggression will simply speed up the annihilation of us all.

Are there alternatives to war? Are there intelligent 'collective' options?

Do Nothing.

This choice, if taken, is perhaps the worst. It reflects the collective resigned mind-state of Man even when opportunity to change really exists. This non-action will indeed result in the removal of Man via our self-made destruction capabilities. *A really unintelligent behaviour.*

Do Something Positive.

Changing historical behaviour by finally recognising that irrespective of race, creed, religion or political leanings or even historical horrors, Man must now work together as one to build a collectively crafted safe path to the future for all our children. This choice, if taken, will demand the complete acceptance that only Man working in the interest of all Man provides the best possible chance in securing a long-term future for humanity. *A really intelligent behaviour.*

Do Something Negative.

This choice will be reflected in the action of one or more Man collectives in a final and last-ditch stupid attempt to prove once and for all that their self-interest and apparently superior way of life is the only correct way to any Man future. Result? War. Utilising the power of the tools of mass destruction against all who are not in agreement with their way. *A really unintelligent behaviour.*

To progress together, sharing all knowledge in science and engineering, remedial medical understanding and maths, building a future world without poverty, without war, without starvation but with freedom of all religious beliefs, freedom of expression through multicultural education, freedom of education, equality for all Man. Respect and recognition for and of the rights of nations, tribes or Man collectives to exist in their own chosen way, as each learns to tolerate all others and take responsibility for the future of all-natural resources. To repair the planet, refreshing the concept of Man in harmony with all that is Mother Nature.

No more propaganda nor 'fake news', no open lies, no manipulation of facts. No unwarm salutations, no unwarm handshakes. Never again should internal population differences within a single society be subjected to manipulation by any other society seeking to acquire or enforce by subversion their own pretences. No individual Man, tribe or collectives shall hold power in any way over others. A 'bully' nation or Man collective must never again be allowed to attempt to enforce its own ideology onto any other.

Building Tomorrow's History Today, Yesterday is Gone.

It is change that we need to make or drown in the abyss of all our historical mistakes. No matter how much we want to look back or shout, it is over, gone, yesterday is nowhere we can ever again belong. So, take a moment to reflect that to survive we have to look forward, treating all Man with mutual respect. It is tomorrow's history we must build with haste or confirm our place as Mother Nature's truest disgrace. Open discussion there has to be attempting to uncover the uniqueness about each other, about you and me.

Once common ground is found, we can debate and then agree a plan to drive us forth, a plan to set us free from our terrible history. A complex task full of shared ideas from

each tribe and clan that works for all the planet's living things, not only Man. No longer shall we tell each other lies nor stand around and criticise but stand together to build a future we all agree that perhaps our great-grandchildren's children may ever see.

Excise all the past hatred with remorse which has brought us to the brink of total disaster, of course. Collectively, we shall seek a way back from the edge of defeat and repair the damage beneath our feet. We have the knowledge, the technical skill, to save ourselves and build anew a world that is free of hate and all ill-will. No need to plan your invasion of our society nor challenge our creed with some other deity. We will never again impose a false piety nor disrespect of others need. Every effort initially will surely be to stop wasting resources for any more mass Man-killing spree. We shall collectively grasp the learning to ensure a better future than our past.

A future our great-grandchildren's children will see, providing opportunity for all to live together in harmony. An impossible dream, I hear you say but is there really any other play that will chase away the horrors of our past? Each of us will share the dream together, working to build a positive future, where Man will live in real peace at last. A dream, no matter how far considered beyond all hope, can be achieved, our differences set aside; we will be able to cope and to abide.

Knowledge, science and technology we can employ for this task diverting abilities used to kill and destroy in the past, preparing the way ahead with innovation and joy. The power to save our planet is in our hands by working together, focused, without fear or panic. Decisions that will have to be made to save this world will need all the resources known to Man. Secrets that were once hidden must be displayed for all to share and all impropriety forgiven.

So much we have to gain along this shared journey path turning our minds to reach out and clasp solutions that will protect us from our past. Clean air we all need to breathe, the plants, the birds, the animals and all the creatures beneath the seas. There has to be a real solution to destroy the pollution levels that our current lifestyles employ. Fossil fuels are the real primary pain turning all industrial and domestic output into acid-rain. Eradicating human misery, starvation and illiteracy will forever be our principal driving force to make all Man free. With common purpose, we can change our behaviour of the past creating a world that will be at last, perhaps, as our forebears wanted for you and for me.

RAS (March 2017)

The Path Ahead

Repairing the sustained damage to our natural environment by Man over many centuries past and present requires rapid urgent attention, not only to stop the damage continuing but also to prevent further future degeneration. Natural physical and atmospheric changes by Mother Nature have always been a regular and common planet phenomenon. An example of such is the ice-ages with their direct cataclysmic effects on changing the topography of the surface while at the same time destroying very many living species. The same applies regarding the impact of volcanic eruptions both on dry land and via the ocean floors. These events, on the one hand, changed life forms but also set the foundation for alternate living matter which acted to refresh the composition of our world.

However, these actions by Mother Nature have not destroyed the earth but may potentially have secured its place in the universe. The primary elements that make up this spinning planet, giving life and sustainability for multitudes of living creatures, continue as before. These events of nature do, of course, create challenges to the surviving species populations and in many cases, forces specific *behaviour* pattern changes. The development of Man and our growth in population, mass killing capabilities and ability to destroy most living species, cannot provide a secure future for this planet.

Man, the apparent primary intelligent species, has the power through its collective nuclear arsenal to inflict a catastrophic physical change to the planet and our atmosphere. This power in the hands of Man cannot be underestimated, not only for its planet destructive potential but also for its Man healing potential. *A tantalising opportunity exists.*

Fear of the unknown in regard to the real outcome of a full-blown nuclear war provides, albeit a reluctant basis, for Man to stop, hesitate, and think. Utilisation of the *knowledge* gathered in the application of such power generation can just as easily be used to provide non-atmospheric polluting energy driving all types of industrial machines including, land, sea, and air transportation across the world. It is this very knowledge that when used in the underdeveloped nations may provide a positive help in speeding up physical developments, from roads to schools, hospitals and the mass production of sustainable foodstuffs of a huge variety. In addition, nuclear energy *knowledge* is increasingly used in the world of medicine. The application of this knowledge across a huge variation of Man endeavours may set the foundation for a collective approach to solving some of the pressing humanitarian, social and atmospheric problems currently encountered.

By redirecting knowledge, technology, money, and of greater importance, time, away from building nuclear bombs, and their delivery systems, towards human social benefit may yet prove to be the one small step for all Man to think today how tomorrow's history will be.

Such an action reflecting behavioural change will confirm that collective Man is on that illusive 'Do Something Positive' path at last. But this is only the beginning of the journey, not the end. Not all will participate due mainly to mistrust and expectation of duplicity as well as continuing the protection of own ideology. Others will jump at the opportunity to participate in the early stages but then enthusiasm may wane due perhaps to tribe, clan or kin, collective disquiet. Speaking out loud on such issues, without fear and not hiding behind them, should always be the approach from now on.

Without full, equal and regular awareness of progress with sharing failures and rewards of successes throughout the initial discussion process between all Man, such misgivings will most certainly arise. Therefore, a full and open dialogue confirming that the way forward is *not* to allow negative impact by any historical cultural beliefs, languages or in any way to discredit any culture or creed but rather to ensure that the eventual outcome will support all Man civilisations. Credibility and trust must be the solid foundation stone of all participants. The collective focus is to build a safe future and cannot be stymied by squabbles about past actions or behaviours. It is now that we are working to save all that currently live and share the planet with us. Here is the most tantalising opportunity. Seeking a methodology for long lasting peace between all.

Using all the knowledge of Man and being totally unencumbered by the past appears to offer a clear possibility for designing the best intelligent way forward to tomorrow's future collectively. Forging jointly a path towards a new world where the very nature of the process will ensure discovery of each other, our strengths and possibilities to achieve a future for Man where recognition of the rights of all Man to live in peace and harmony transcends all cultural, creed, race or religious differences. Instead, a joint recognition to work for the continuing and combined improvement of all of Earth's living wonders. Exploring together the innovations that technology, through the sharing of knowledge, can bring.

That human life holds the key, the primary essence yet to come. This responsibility rests with Man today, to build tomorrow's history today through our children.

Can we build for our children's tomorrow?

They Are Tomorrow

You are born from darkness into the light
You are colours all of this world with sight
You are observing using un-focusing eyes
You are movement not being recognised.

You are love and trust all rolled into one
You are vacant, really yearning to belong
You are life anew and opportunity for us
You are tears of joy without any mistrust

You are laughter untainted, no corruption
You are sleep, no need for an interruption
You are happiness held close to give bliss
You are hope for a world near to an abyss

You are pupil learning to count and read
You are student seeing changes we need
You are adult now wishing to participate
You are politics, open, just dealing straight.

You are warm, caring for every yesteryear
You are music fully in tune, always so clear
You are reason with appreciation of myth
You are loyal and always trusting herewith

You are old, facing your final act of this play
You are clean, humble unashamed of today
You are warrior, not afraid of truth nor pain
You are peace allowing others to live again.

You are human, proffering help without gain
You are tolerance, respect established again
You are over no more to leave do or renew
You are past no more can you say or do but…we are not you.

They Are the Future

They are born from darkness into the light
They are colours all of this world with sight.
They are future, where we shall not belong
They are thankful for all that we have done.

They are love and trust all rolled into one
They are welcomed are needed to belong.
They are life anew with opportunity for all
They are tears of joy, learning how to crawl.

They are laughter, untainted, no corruption
They are sleep no need for an interruption.
They are happiness held close to give bliss
They are hope for the future world not this.

They are pupils learning to count and read
They are students building what they need.
They are wiser than who ever came before
They are real in truth no disguising anymore.

They are warm fully caring for any yesteryear
They are music playing in tune always so clear.
They are reason but not afraid to accept myth
They are loyal, love, forever trusting herewith.

They are old, accepting a final act of their play
They are truth clean, unashamed of their day.
They are warriors, unafraid of true deep pain
They are peace so that all others can live again.

They are human, proffering help without gain
They are tolerance, all respect built to remain
They are over, no more to leave do or renew
They are past no more can they say or do but...
Man has a future true

That's Wicked (or Is It?)

When you were small, growing up, do you remember being a little scared of any imaginary ghosts like a 'bogeyman' or goblin hiding under your bed? Were there nursery rhymes that sounded funny but frightened you with whispers of monster stories that you recall? If so, can you remember being distressed, perhaps causing loss of sleep or fright and panicky nervous moments? How did you react to that sudden 'bump' in the night? If indeed you do recall these times, have you ever thought that like so very many before you, you may have been subjected to these scary moments as a result of parents, siblings or other family members reciting children's nursery rhymes perhaps, leaving you with a quiet unease? Has it never, at any time when older, occurred to you that these were all part of your specific society's child-management indoctrination?

Every Man society throughout history has created these 'un-real' imaginings as a part of instilling in all its citizens, especially when children, an awareness that if you say or do the apparently 'wrong' thing or not do something that your parents or society is requiring of you, these scary things may seek you out as some sort of punishment. In some societies across this world, the male child for instance, is regarded as a supremely important gift while the female child is seen of lesser importance. Apparent rhymes and or scary stories lay the foundation in each gender of a tribe, clan or Man collective, to create a strong fundamental character and behaviour difference between genders.

Again, this is simply preparing the youngsters to the ways of a particular society or cultural style. Perhaps also this may have been reflective of the possible important 'use' of a male human in terms of defence, protection, strength and required stamina. Nevertheless, such behaviour may have pre-set the foundation of the male child to recognise that females may be of lesser importance within that particular society. The division of human children by identifying them as of greater or lesser importance based on gender, endures in many societies across the world today. Such 'scary' tactics used are not just silly nonsense play time or sleep time fun things. They are employed often without realisation of their true purpose by parents, teachers, religious leaders or older siblings.

Designed to shape child-awareness that rules do apply for your inclusion into the community. This methodology of subliminal population control has been deployed for generations upon generations. Its purpose is to plant a familiarity of 'our community rules' of kinship. Today still in certain African tribes, for example, the males must face a challenge of strength, of cunning and purpose, or ability to 'bloody-their-sword' prior to acceptance into manhood.

Some similar Man tribes follow well established traditions in expecting a female child to 'prove' ability to produce offspring at a very early age. This may then enhance their 'value' in the event of marriage at a future date. In others, girls are denied the opportunity of academic schooling and must work alongside the adult females of their community, usually in the gathering and preparation of food for the important 'men-folk'. As a child, then, the female will learn from an early age that male children are special.

The following is dedicated to the life of an unknown sixteen-year old girl in Pakistan. Forgive the innocent!

Come Brother, help kill my daughter (yet another 'honour' killing)

A beautiful flower born that day just sixteen years ago, so very full of infant life,
A female child giving instant love to those around her, naked, unaware of strife.
Unfocused eyes this baby girl had as arms reach out to find a mother's first hug,
Her father stands bowing his head in shame. A girl! He slinks away with a shrug.

Raised by her mother in all expected behaviour and beliefs, she learns the rules
To obey, without pause, hold respect for elders, excluded from going to school.
Village life embraces another poor girl, accepting her future will be as planned
By her family, with no input from her, Just obedience. All objections are banned.

A childhood offering little opportunity allowing no self-expression or life choice,

So, as time passed, she made friends with other quiet girls
living without a voice.
She found one special friend to share giggling with laughing
and time for a smile,
Growing up together standing in the sun, holding secret
dreams if just for a while.

She was a sixteen-year old girl, obedient, having fun with a
friend she held dear,
Her family was kind, though strict, but she found a quiet
way to live without fear.
Her special friend said she was reading, learning of the big
world, all around her,
Descriptions of some other beliefs, of shining, living
colours, making her unsure.

Then, at almost seventeen, her trusted friend confided in her
of a love she held
For a village boy, not her parents' chosen one. Why has she
to feel so compelled?
Shattering the rules of forced innocence, she spoke of a one
love so strong in her,
Knowing she has to follow her lover's shared dream. Escape
now, today or never!

Calmly they plan an escape for the girl and her young love,
to seek a better land
Once planned, her friend turned, offering her thanks for
that friendly steady hand.
Saying their fond farewells each held the other, knowing the
dangers in their task,

This was challenging each family's status-quo, shattering their illusions of the past.

The father who sixteen years ago slunk away with a shrug, it was just another girl,
Learned of his daughter's rule betrayal putting his family in disgrace, life in a whirl.
He called upon his daughter to explain, stating their family honour must be saved
A debt, now owed by them to the family of her friend, a debt that has to be paid.

Meeting with the elders, he discussed what must be done to repair family honour,
Crying tears of fear or shame, it was agreed he was not to blame for such a horror.
Considering his plea, the elders agreed the girl must die now to set her family free,
This will take away the debt, saving the family honour as done throughout history.

Sat with the elders is the brother of the father, the young girl's uncle, eyes-smiling,
Her father kneeling in relief, requests the elders guide to carry out this deed crying.
'Come Brother to me', he hears, "together we shall rebuild our family honour today,"
Our actions in public view will restore our pride, rid us of this debt we have to pay.

Together they plan her death and used a hanging tree,
where she is hung until dead,
A notice for all to see that rules must always be obeyed, or
consequences are dread
A pyre built beneath is lit for disposing of their troubles,
smoothing their road ahead.
With the debt now paid, honour so restored, the families
share a gathering to talk,
Of the elders blessing, releasing them all from their debt,
just as they were taught!

May 2016—National British daily, page 27:
'Yet another honour killing in Pakistan'
Village elders arrested along with the father and uncle of
the sixteen-year-old girl who was murdered (all were
released, insufficient evidence to prosecute!).

RAS (weeping) June 2016

In all societies, the passing down of specific clan values
and behaviours begins with spoken words or fantasy stories,
designed to start the assimilation of the recipient child into its
community. Such indoctrination of a society can also be
found in patriotic music composed to put 'fire-in-the-belly' of
the listeners. National Anthems epitomise this when music is
directed to support particular Man collectives, proud or
sombre moment.

The United Kingdom 1902 AD patriotic song 'Land of
Hope and Glory' is a great example. However, the words of
this song raise potentially hard questions to answer today. The
music was written by Edward Elgar as part of a larger piece

for the coronation of Edward V11. The coronation date was set for the 26th of June 1902. On hearing the music, Edward V11 suggested that this particular section would make a 'good song'. He asked A.C. Benson, a poet, if he could put words to the tune and 'Land of Hope and Glory' was the result. The most popular 'British' rousing song is still played today on the last night of the proms each year. Is this wicked?

The Words

*Land of **hope** and **glory**, Mother of the **free***
How shall we extol thee who are born of thee?
***Wider** still and wider shall thy **bounds** be set*
***God** who made thee mighty make thee mightier yet.*
God who made thee mighty make thee mightier yet.

The Time 1902

The 2nd Boer War ended on the 31st of May 1902.

The major *hope* at the time was in the hearts of the mothers, fathers, brothers, sisters, wives and children of the mainly conscripted 350,000 UK soldiers sent to fight in the 2nd Boer War in South Africa. Their *Hope* was that their loved ones returned unharmed. The same *hope* existed in the colonies for the 150,000 colonial 'volunteers'. *Hope* at the time in the general UK population was for a better future in the new century. Such expressions indicate that the past may have lacked any feeling of *hope* among the ordinary UK citizens.

Total Boer forces were just over 40,000 of which some 6,200 were dead and 24,000 prisoners had been shipped to

POW camps in several UK colonies. UK losses were just over 22,000 dead, nearly 950 missing and almost 23,000 wounded.

Civilian casualties in South Africa were just over 46,000 of which '26,370 were Boer women and children' who died mainly of starvation in concentration camps establish by the British. In addition, some *20,000 Black Africans* died of starvation in separate concentration camps.

Not a lot of **glory** to sing about there by the British at all!

Oh yes, the winning of this war secured ownership by the British of enormous mineral wealth due to the recent discovery of one of the largest gold, diamond, uranium and platinum deposits in the world. More massive wealth for the British empire to exploit!

Wider still and **Wider** is regarded by some as a reference to the fact that Cecil Rhodes, a champion of the Victoria era of empire expansion in South Africa, in his will, bequeathed a considerable personal fortune to be used to promote the 'extension of British rule throughout the world'. He apparently provided a long list of countries/territories which he wanted to be colonised and placed under British rule.

For the word **Bounds**, read boundaries, reflecting the desire to expand the British empire of the day even further, little caring for what the human cost may be.

The absolute and unforgivable claim that it was "**God** who made (thee/British/us) mighty…" is how the British leaders of the era disclaim any responsibility for the centuries of murderous pillaging and raping of other Man collectives across the world. "It wasn't us see it was *God*." Such was the belief in this that the line is the only one in the song to be repeated!

Such songs do, though, seek to arouse feelings of togetherness, standing side by side in the face of any real or imagined adversity or triumph. In the developed countries of our planet, education of all children is generally seen today as a fundamental principle. There do remain Man societies in nations across the planet where this is not the case. Mass education in the developed countries though has only been in existence for a very relatively short time. Yes, there have been centres of education and learning across very many Man societies over hundreds or even thousands of years but recipients of these facilities where reliant on family lineage or power-status or religious participation. These students only ever represented a minute number of the population where such activities took place.

The great masses of populations, irrespective of location tribe or clan did not receive any education…other than clan rules, fables and propaganda. The latter was always designed to constantly reinforce culture, structure and status as being a direct privilege of and by the consequence of birth. Born into the elite or the very lowly was just an accident of nature and nothing to do with any capacity of the new born to learn, do, or contribute to the society as a whole.

European societies were generally forced to change their education structure shortly after the arrival of the industrial age. For thousands of years prior to the industrial revolution the masses in most countries worked and lived off the land. Not owners of the land but as growers of crops, keepers of livestock while living in small enclaves or on the land of the strong and powerful wealthy.

People born into these communities would seldom have an opportunity to move from the environment into which they were born. If close enough, they may have enjoyed an opportunity to visit the nearest similar settlement. If not, they remained growing up in the same community, getting married and producing offspring.

Large families were demanded of the time because life-span was generally not long. Inter-marriages often resulted in bringing additional human challenges.

Most people spent their lives working in the fields, worshipping in their local community church in a language they mostly could not understand and survived on a hand-to-mouth poverty level, generation upon generation. The males were regarded by the elite, the leaders, the lords and masters as essential 'cannon-fodder' for use in local as well as distant Man to Man conflict whenever needed. However, requirement for mass employment caused by the industrial revolution resulted in 'workers' migrating in large numbers from the land into employment in factories, foundries, down the coal mines or in the mills.

'Going-to-work' caused the creation of more towns with less and less people living in the former farming settlements. Machines ruled. Steel foundries pumped out a multitude of ever-changing products to support the ever-changing and growing demand. 10-year-old boys joined their father 'down-the-pit' to help haul coal to the surface. All the time the gap between those with access to academic education and those without rapidly increased.

Until the late 18th and early 19th century it was recognised that this 'gap' of available basic education should be addressed. In the United Kingdom the Church of England and the Roman Catholic Church in England and across Europe, played a leading role in the creation of schools for the children of their village or town locations. Each such institution would however colour the subject content of their teachings to reflect their own thoughts and doctrine. Wealthy business owners supported these efforts although the 'learning period' was initially only between ages 5 years to 11 years. It was soon recognised, though, that education for all children across many countries in Europe was becoming the key to a nation's economic future. Each country had by the late 19th century established its own mass education programme and this created a foundation for continued industrial growth.

By the end of the 19th century, compulsory education had become a standard in many European and developed countries.

But...

Many, if not all, national education systems contained inaccurate behavioural characteristics and pious illusions through the favourable colouring of their historical behaviour to both their own and other Man collectives across the world. Historical, in this instance, means stretching back from yesterday all the way to the beginning of that nation or tribe or clan.

Propaganda hid many ugly truths of European colonial exploitation. Reference to the plundering of physical resources, wealth and power across so many continents often accompanied with the slaughter of local populations and bludgeoning the survivors into subservient status. Such realisms were simply not reflected as in the past behaviours of 'our' tribe, clan or nation. The expounding of glorious heroics of the nation's efforts for its people, though, are obvious and oh so many. However, truth of past horrific deeds of invasion, plundering and pillaging for the glory of themselves are, to some degree, much more obvious by their very absence both in print and spoken word.

Inaccurate flowering of such behaviour and associated political or elite protectionism enveloped the education of children in most countries or nations in a cocoon of comfortable falsehood. The result? When argument and conflict, real or wanted, needed war, the men and boys of the population masses became the cannon-fodder.

Mass population education programmes have failed, to a large degree, in the objective of maintaining a national self-warmth and cosy consistency of its historical past behaviours. This remains directly due to the awakening of the minds of the masses via the education programmes themselves. Minds in knowledge generated questions and where answers were given each was subjected to challenge, seeking out the truth independently and, of course, exposing through questioning the propaganda-filled national historic perspectives.

Fake news can be seen as perhaps a last-ditch attempt of those wishing to maintain divisions of population by class, religion, sexual or political orientation. The implementation of education systems across all learning subjects including religious teachings in these countries carried a national bias of character to infuse mass warmth and pride among its citizens. Suddenly perceived piety and social success of these nations created public demand to know how? When? From where?

By the middle of the 20th century, and following two world wars, education in the developed world countries remained somewhat partisan. As time passed into the last quarter, though, pupil populations assisted with the advent of fast and popular communications as well as intercontinental travel opportunities, started to recognise the falsehoods and began the seeking out of real truth. By the late 20th century, the structured bias in many education programmes had been identified and amended. Yes, history is amendable, shades of one George Orwell. The application of real knowledge-based learning thereafter played a significant and innovative influence in the rapid growth and use of computer technology in all areas of learning and employment. This progress has seen continuous new discoveries.

Much of this, for example, identified the environmental destructive elements across the world generated by Man during the industrial revolution. New and broader knowledge acquired via extensive education programmes running into the 21st century have created a fluid platform that drives fast changes, with the result that the developed countries in the world are moving further and further away from those remaining in the industrial, or in some cases, agricultural, periods.

That enormous gap previously existing between a tiny number of a population in education and the rest, which had existed for so very long, was now closed for good in the developed nations.

As a direct result of the expansion of education several specific behaviour changes of the 'general public' in these countries have already taken place. Bland acceptance of official printed publications, government decree, political expectations or stated fact is now something of the past. The masses no longer accept and follow like sheep but instead constantly challenge such utterances.

Democracy is no longer the privilege of the high and wealthy. Succession of the elite is no longer guaranteed.

Politicians can, and are, cast asunder with stunning regularity. Some due to anti-social behaviour or pure dim-wittedness. When one considers that it was just over one hundred and fifty years ago in England when only those male members of high society or of wealth, favour and standing were allowed to vote. A tiny number of men. Not then a real or open democracy at all. The elite retained full power. Demands for change remained constant and many but it was not until 1867 that working-class male householders, property owners, in cities and towns were also allowed to vote. This was followed by several changes and amendments over the next 50 years until finally in 1918, following the First World War and possibly as a 'gift' to appease those returning from the horror of war, universal voting rights were awarded to all adult male citizens of the UK population.

As is well documented, all adult females, citizens of the same population were finally granted universal suffrage ten years later in 1928. This followed the initial 1918 provision for women aged 30 years and above and being property owners. This power-shift to the general populace in England, linked with developing education for all now ensured that a more comprehensive open and democratic doctrine was fully established.

Similar progress in the area of population universal suffrage was made in many western European countries. Each adopted its own type of parliamentary structures, voting franchise and governing agenda. However, in the 21st century so far, it is evident that demands are again arising across many of these established economies for something different but, as yet, not fully defined. Remnants of the old order cling to their diminishing status often hampering progress towards a more innovative approach of national varying political franchise discussions and progress.

As always, at times in the past with the awakening of a new vision or order driven by the populace, turbulence and unease currently simmer in a number of the so-called developed countries.

This has been reflected in 'unexpected' results of several general elections in some of the major economies in the world. New alliances are being formed both domestically and, in some cases, internationally. Former collective accords on such vital world issues as climate-change and international business trading customs are being challenged and reviewed. All this is taking place as these nations move into a future hi-tech knowledge-based economy.

Will the 'developed' nations of the current era be proud of the legacy being created for future generations? As machines and hi-tech take over the majority of mass production of goods and services resulting in the loss of mass Man employment opportunities, will education changes meet the future skills needed to support all Man? With the expected massive population growth across the world during this century, will individual life chances exist for equal opportunity to grow and prosper? Will the slow to learn and or re-learn, the infirm and unbalanced become a new massive majority? Can the closed education availability gap in the developed nations provide support to the underdeveloped nations?

Time to think differently is now.
Time to behave differently is now.
Time to learn from each other is now.

Time to seek a collective way towards a better future for all Man is now.

Time, say so many, is running out.

Pushing Towards Tomorrow

The only hope for real true change is that you never look behind. Because that is what it has been, it cannot change your mind. There are no fixed or solid answers yet to be secured or matched. They sit deep within each and every one of you simply waiting to be hatched. We of the past were misguided, lost in ignorance of any harmless future choice. But you have opportunity to build anew with everyone exploring tomorrow using a single voice! Poverty of millions will never fade away unless you use all resources to create a new and lasting way.

War and killing has never been the answer so be open, honest, no more hurtful lies to say. You hold in your hands a worldwide opportunity for the creation of a brand-new human day. A future sharing knowledge must be your aim with humanity beside you recognising at last that you are all the same. Go on, be brave and reach out to all others to find peace and shared prosperity without the need for any shame. The cynics will be yelling from the side-lines so bring them in one by one, show them openly what progress you have made, what has already been done.

Recover human dignity in and across all creeds, always looking forwards knowing together that so much more can be achieved. Follow all the visions lighting the way ahead seeking out a positive future path along which all Man can tread. Here there is the answer, where love shall be the guide to a world full of options while humanity walk side by side. Then, in shared adventure, the universe is yours to explore! Discover the galaxies together for the next millennia and more.

Record your truth in guidance for those who follow on from you creating a shared history of the future for all to hold pure and true. A safe way to build tomorrow's future history is remembering it is too late to build that of today.

RAS (June 2017)

Anyone Seen the Devil?

That non-existent wicked being. That fictitious something that apparently hides out amongst us all. When as children, we were subjected to unsavoury or frightening nursery rhymes, as we grew older, this illusive 'being' was persistently identified as the purveyor of all things bad. Always the opposite of good. Such a thing (devil) is referenced across all Man superstitions or irrational beliefs and survives as the adult Man cover-up phenomena for the atrocious behaviour of Man itself. Blame the devil for all Man lies, self-inflicted cruelty, cheating, drug-taking, greed, gluttony, prostitution and abuse of the weak the poor and the unwell.

When holy men of the Roman Catholic Church identified people as witches during the European dark ages, such unfortunates were burnt to death in public, by the same 'holy' men! Was this the devil at play? When an estimated 28,000 men and boys were slaughtered in just twelve hours on Palm Sunday at the battle of Towton in Yorkshire during the English War of the Roses in 1461 AD, was the devil at play? Was the devil having fun in the building of gas chambers to kill millions of Man in Europe during the Second World War or at the Aberfan disaster in Wales in 1966 AD? Must it always be the devil at play when any physical abuse of any Man by any other Man takes place?

In my reality, the devil, or its equivalent in other creeds and languages, is just the excuse used by and for all Man to bury their own evil. At the same time, it is used as a scare tactic, so that if an individual's behaviour or beliefs are not in line with 'ours', such individual, or indeed Man collective, will reside for ever in some form of purgatory. All others supporting our creed will move on to an ecstatic glory. So, is the use of this non-Man-thing wicked? The fact is that in any society the strong of will or voice or persuasion in the collective will dominate. The timid, shy and weak will shrink away to find solace when faced with challenge from the strong. Those with apparent power will then strengthen their position challenging all other pretenders to their status so that the elite of the initial strong have control.

This is accepted and recognised in 'wild' animal behaviour, of course. Such power and status must then be defended protecting own society rules which were created mainly to maintain the status-quo. Those at the top define the future for all, until defeated. Is there possibly any other way for Man?

Why not, for example, simply agree that the lifestyle, society rules, creeds, politics and all differing hocus-pocus of all Man tribes, clans, collective or nations on this planet have the right to exist in the fashion they choose? Providing such life style choice is not aggressive toward, or invasive of, any other Man collective but works in harmony with all others in a united drive to secure a better long-term future for the planet and all living issue of Mother Nature.

The two sentences above each contain a depiction that seems an impossibility for Man to achieve. Is this inability also wicked?

Sometimes the devil is apparently seen as something of a general quirk in all that is the nature of the planet or universe. A foible that mysteriously leads Man to and into evil. Something in the stars perhaps, or a corruption of the elements around a particular weather season. This nonentity also, apparently, has a big boss to whom he reports, just like any junior soldier. His name? Satan! Has anyone seen this Satan boss-thing, this so-called principal chief of all evil?

Such is the deep and overpowering influence of this boss of all evil in the life of Man and in particular the English language and grammar rules so that in order to write his given name here…**it must start with a capital 'S'!** Yet in the previous paragraph, every reference to the devil (as here) has no such high-status requirement. Oh, the corrupted influence and power of indoctrination. While god can be written either God or as at the beginning of the sentence, does this imply that god therefore is not of equal-status? Surely such difference between these two mystic-beings is an insult? Well at least to one of them?

The reference above to these incorporeal myths, these Man imagined *things*, is my way of exposing that consistent escapology capability Man has deployed to manage their clan and kin to ensure subordination through ignorance and fear. This same principle is used today to strengthen leaders hold over the docile in many nations across our planet. Such Man behaviour continues to admonish the very concept that an educated population will, can, and increasingly does, challenge the former status-quo seeking to drive out 'truth' above any other demand. Such global challenge of the 'old order' has, as yet, no single or collective leader.

However, the voices of the many are clambering towards exposing the non-truth of the past. Challenge is not to pursue retribution but to gain real collective acceptance through knowledge, as the basis to move forward in building an alternative Man behaviour style. Not only is obvious former propaganda exposed but also this exposure of the truth provides a sound foundation on which to tackle the development of an alternative future together.

Treading the new knowledge-based path into tomorrow may not provide all the answers. There will be multiple pitfalls on the way forward. However, the rewards for the security of Man generations yet to come demands such a journey is undertaken now. Without progress, no matter how slow or difficult Man future will remain bleak. The rewards for sharing the hazards in reaching a collective understanding and respect of each other will surely result in a much better world. If humanity working together proves impossible, shall our collective consciences place the blame on that nasty non-man, the devil, as we go about the task of self-annihilation? The easy option of doing nothing to change us, will result in just that. The most difficult challenge is to change our basic behaviour.

What would Russia gain in invading Europe? Or China, or the United States of America?

What would Iran gain in invading Iraq? Or Afghanistan or Turkey?

What would be gained if the United Kingdom invaded Argentina? Or Germany, or Iceland?

What would China gain by invading Japan? Or Russia, or Mongolia?

The reality is that such action by any country attacking any other at this time in Man history can only result in hastening the demise of all current civilisations. Even with the approval of the UN for rapid intervention in some sort of valiant attempt to protect the non-protagonist nations, the outcome is very likely to be the same. Royalty and/or wealthy 'families' fighting family members, cousins, brothers or any variations no longer exists. Using all the males in their kingdoms to fight and to kill or be killed in their role of subservient beings is of the past. Education and knowledge, technology, science and engineering have ensured that the once 'conscript' able males of the community no longer live in total ignorance. It is now opposing Man collective alliances supporting each other that can and will destroy Man.

Can Man avoid this by sharing knowledge, wealth and building respect for all others? Some may be cautious, others may be really enthusiastic, still others will demand that it is done. Many will hold back unaccepting that knowledge sharing may help secure Man's future. The military in each existing Man tribe, clan or collectives, will likely scream, along with the worlds gun-runners, for their 'job security'. What an irony that would be! The caretakers of those national secrets must surrender to the loss of their false, diabolical stature of misguided importance. The historical ill-gotten funds of the wealthy could be surrendered to benefit all Man in their shared search for a meaningful secure future.

Oh, but what of the cost of such an endeavour? A working Man community in shared peace and common direction aiming to build tomorrows history today? Is it too impossible to achieve acceptance and mutual respect for each other as we step into tomorrow?

The drive must initially be to construct a peaceful long-term coexistence and cooperation for and of all. A task without pre-judgment or definition of the end result. A task where achievement or failure will only be measured by those whom the participants shall never meet, the children of the future.

Will our grandchildren's great-grandchildren, if we allow them to exist, look back on us of the early 21st century with pride?

The year is 2101 in the 22nd century. CE, officially.

(Version 1)

The giant passenger space ship settled softly onto the no 17 arrivals pad almost an hour earlier than its scheduled arrival time. It took just a few moments for the aerial connecting corridors to lock onto the ship allowing all 2,500 passengers to commence their disembarkation simultaneously. The complete journey from Earth to the reception centre on the moon had taken just 7 hours.

On arrival at the reception centre, the tourists, some on their way to various holiday hotels, while others were returning home, all transferred to their assigned local transport systems. These included those needing flights out to several hotels set in constant orbit in space as well as those near to the historical site of the first Man landing on the moon in 1969. Looking up towards earth through the glass ceiling of the aerial corridors, all first-time visitors marvel at the blue earth atmosphere and its glowing clarity.

The World Governing Body (WGB), with representatives of every Man society on earth, had achieved so much due to the outstanding measure of cooperation of all Man, irrespective of differences. Each knowledge-sharing Man society providing specialists to very many of the collective projects undertaken following the first quarter of the 21st century. One of the largest such projects was that of securing clean air linked to retarding the rapid heat increase of the worldwide self-inflicted global-warming crisis. This was a most successful task resulting in full management of the issues leading to the ability to identify any further threats of increase.

Other major projects included huge infrastructure projects across the planet using clean renewable energy which ensured continued support of all earth-bound life. Science in all its aspects, in association with engineering innovation has made startling leaps forward in all forms of travel, building materials, health and education. In addition, in 2022, all countries signed an agreement to reduce spending on military equipment and defence at the rate of 20 percent of their 2020 actuals, every 5 years. The first such period was at year-end 2027 AD (CE) then at the end of each successive 5th year period thereafter. Any country not complying with this would have been suspended from the WGB forum and placed under the direct management of a WGB specialist team to help them reach each target date.

Much of this former military expenditure was diverted into education, where wanted, benefiting millions of Man and ensuring that the security of the planet and all its living inhabitants became an integral part of a peaceful future-plan. Defence spending after the completion of this agreed reduction period has been under the absolute control of the WGB. Much is currently used in developing defence capability from potential inter-planetary hostility.

A matter of much debate as no confirmation has yet been received that aliens do actually exist. For the purposes of expediency, however, a large number of possibilities are being explored. Protection from natural space events are included in this research and development area.

Advances in scientific research and cooperation across the world has enabled Man to create clean-energy factories in space, as well as on earth, which have reduced earth-bound fossil fuel negative atmospheric output to nil. New human colonies are already established on the moon as well as Mars and plans are in place for further planetary exploration during the years ahead. Over the last few decades medical research has successfully resulted in many new drugs being manufactured in space laboratories, with abilities to eradicate most common Man illnesses. This includes all types of diabetic disorders and many types of different cancers. DNA string research has seen the capability of rectifying some major genetic disorders. New health benefit discoveries are almost an annual occurrence.

Research laboratories are operating in many areas of Mars investigating local supplies of natural underground minerals and chemical deposits. At the beginning of this year, the total number of Man, living and working off-Earth reached just over 17,000 and is well above the initial target established in 2065 of 12,000. Growth of the current number continues unabated as new opportunities arise almost daily.

While Man to Man conflict still exists on occasion, open discussion on arguments and differences are generally resolved without military intervention. The collective awareness of the elected members of the WGB is always available to work with all parties involved in seeking the best possible solution. The massive loss of life via Man to Man conflicts of the 20th and the first quarter of the 21st centuries has not been repeated. In fact, this has been reduced to the occasional inter-society squabbling.

The power of a member country of the WGB is freedom of self-government, religious expression, society rules and structure. Management of own resources, clan and society remain absolutely intrinsic to each country. It is the citizens of each country who determine its own community behaviours towards each other. In recognition of respect for the right to life, each member of the WGB has agreed to honour and respect the right of all religions, peoples, sects and societies. There still remain very many controversial activities in some societies across the planet but these are subject only to the jurisdiction of each of such societies, not any other. All are welcome to seek advice and help via open discussion with the WGB should they want to amend their particular society culture in any way.

The reforestation of earth is completed and it was confirmed recently that the plankton levels of the oceans on earth have been fully restored. The use of non-biodegradable plastics has been banned for many years now together with the complete eradication of the internal combustion engine. All earth-bound transport is now powered by renewable electricity or protected nuclear energy. Dealing with nuclear waste, however, remains a difficult challenge. The quality of sunlight travelling through space itself is just one research project identified by the solar energy and nuclear scientists as perhaps opportunity to move away from the use of nuclear power completely. This, in particular, is a major opportunity in the propulsion needs for space travel.

Anti-gravity transportation research is beginning to see some future deployment possibilities. However, it is expected to be many years yet before such a transportation method is wide-spread. Over 60 percent of all previous arable crops grown on Earth are produced hydroponically now with the resultant massive land saving being used to build homes, fisheries, natural woodlands and habitats for as many wild flowers, insects and animals as possible.

Large areas on Earth, formally regarded as arid lands or barren wastes, are now used as multicultural university towns and cities accommodating studies on an ever-increasing array of subjects in every language. Students from all Man societies attend, work and study together. This ensures opportunity for cross cultural understanding of society choices by students from all Man countries irrespective of creed, colour, political and social structures. Students from all areas of the planet first explore their differences, learn from them, share acceptance of them, driving away the propaganda and myths, allowing personal opportunity freedom to explore innovations together. The speed of the open dialogue between them has produced amazing social benefits in and across all Man endeavours.

The WGB is currently developing a collective strategy for further space exploration across our galaxy now that most spacecraft are currently being designed, constructed and tested on several space stations within both Earth and Mars orbits. The mining of exciting new minerals found on a number of comets has provided excellent discoveries of new raw materials and confidence is very high that we are not too far away from using these in all areas of mass goods production.

The parents of every individual born today are offered the opportunity for each child to be electronically tagged. To provide warnings via remote and local interface capabilities on a range of possible genetic medical ailments as well as possible non-generic infections, diseases and common illnesses.

This allows for constant monitoring of the health of such individual citizens of Man. In its very early stages of course, there was a large amount of suspicion and fear of the possibility of misuse. Nevertheless, the management of the health of the entire Man population, not just the few is one of the 4 Man benefit cornerstones of the WGB.

The others are 'inter-culture freedom', allowing all who wish to explore one or all other cultures to do so without hindrance, providing that such activity is to seek understanding and learning. The 'Non-Military Action Plan' provides that without the agreement of the WGB any attempt to use military force of any kind will result in the suspension of the parties and direct intervention of the WGB. The fourth is the 'Access to Truth'. This is designed to ensure that open, frank and honest dialogue by each living Man to any other is a right, ensuring that attempts at propaganda or undermining truth are easy to identify and stop. This cornerstone ensures freedom of expression for all Man.

Although the expected Man population growth in the first decade of the Last century suggested that by this year, 2101, it would be close to 11 billion, the current population is just reaching 9.7 billion. This is reportedly due, in part, to the sharing of knowledge, and much has been done on the reduction of poverty levels in the areas previously known as the 'underdeveloped nations'. The WGB programme of building a united fight against ignorance and poverty in all such areas has proven to be a real community development success. There is now substantial enthusiasm across these nations to ensure a constant exchange of ideas in self-sufficiency and population planning with the rest of the world.

So, at the beginning of this new 22nd century, space exploration, harmless sustainable energy sources and the growth in shared knowledge has significantly amended so many of past Man behaviours. There's still some way to go but this human species looks set to secure a long-term state of actuality. Those of us today bringing up the next generation and the one after that, fully agree that the future holds a generosity of Man possibilities yet to be defined.

We in this new century live and work to secure the betterment of all Man who follow on from us. As in the past, we will make mistakes, some of which may place terrible burdens on our great-grandchildren. Nevertheless, we are proud of our forefathers for their acknowledgement that without significant behavioural changes, we may not be living as we are today.

The year is 2101 in the 22nd century CE.

(Version 2)

Our water filtering system has broken down, again!

The water-level gauge on our sealed isolation tank is showing us that just 11 percent of the normal total volume is available. As there are currently 375 people in our clan, with rationing, we may be able to stretch this out over the next 17 days. This is yet another emergency issue and one which, if not corrected, has the potential to kill us all. Without access to a decontaminated water supply we will have no choice but to travel to the nearest surviving community seeking help. There is, however, no certainty that they are not also experiencing a similar issue. If indeed they are, there will, without doubt, be reluctance to share whatever water they have.

The system filtering the raw water being drawn up from deep below the surface has been indicating for over two weeks that a fault has occurred. The local community authority has ignored our advice and request for help, delivered by our officially recognised clan messenger. We will very soon need to break the principle civil rule of 'stay put' or face the possibility of extinction. Over the last thirty years, our clan has been able to secure the growth of sufficient arable crops below ground in a former church crypt. Here, the roof above, or as previously known, the vestry floor, remains intact, providing for shelter from direct weather contamination above while the very thick supporting walls underground have also prevented potential contamination.

In this same environment, we have managed also to support the survival of a small number of fruit trees and berry bushes. However, pollination has proven to be the biggest challenge here. This has been done with moderate success by clan members who are constantly monitoring the health of these. These too may now die, even though we deploy very little water here.

Had our great-grandparents been able to avoid what was to be a catastrophic conflict towards the end of the first half of the last century, we know our lives would be so different today. However, we survive. With just a small number of Man in our clan today, which was over 600 just 20 years ago, the possibility of long-term existence for the remaining community is now very slim indeed. The stillbirth rate of our children is almost 70%, all of which, it is suggested, is as a direct result of the atmospheric poisoning from those terrible events just over 53 years ago.

It is, of course, possible that the local community authority, in receipt each year of individual clan member numbers, may now consider the investment required in the delivery of energy and decontaminated water to us may best be used elsewhere. The rule, as we understand it, is to ensure that other larger clans have a better chance for long-term survival than small communities. In the past 7 years, no less than 11 clans, each of less than 150 members in several nearby settlement areas, have been taken off the communal survival support service. Without the vital supply of decontaminated water, they have either been killed in attempting to steal from other clans or, as is often the case, they agree a collective suicide pact to avoid the rigours of a death by toxic atmospheric poisoning.

The rate of human tissue corruption is known to be slow but once it commences there is no medication to ease the long painful journey to the end. Yes, each clan must abide by the civil rule to 'stay put'. Any attempt to join another nearby clan may result in them being killed, perhaps even on the orders of the local community authority. Such a rule, although extreme, has ensured that each clan cannot attack or be attacked by any other. This is irrespective of life style needs or emergences commonly experienced. Our overall agreed survival community plan is that all knowledge on all matters regarding the successful creation of all local clans will eventually provide for the creation of a one nation state of survivors. However, very few Man remain today living in any state that resembles life as it was before the events of just over 50 years ago.

The conflagration destruction across almost all the former primary mass populated countries has resulted in the creation of a corruption of Mother earth resulting in a no-go toxic band around the earth. The term 'Middle Earth' now refers to and covers a massive molten swathe running in a broad band that is reportedly thousands of miles wide. Recent confirmation has been obtained, following the reinstated ability to send and receive radio voice messages, that there are many northern communities of Man that are known to exist in the relatively safe areas above this liquefied mess.

In addition, it is suggested that the Man survival numbers are much greater in the far south than those here in the north. So, in reality, the home planet of Man is now divided by a giant lethal belt. Just how many survivors there are is not yet fully known in either hemisphere. The last known Man population of earth before the 'event' was reported as approximately 8 billion.

Current speculation, which is pure guesswork without any foundation in this year 2101, is said to be about 2 billion. It is hoped that we may soon know the real figures of the Man population as communications systems become more powerful. The task of rebuilding a civilisation is very far away from our life needs. It is the simple things such as access to decontaminated clean water, shelter from the constant bitter cold, safe food of any sort and trying to educate our offspring who make it past the age of five years, on how to survive.

There is teaching of reading and writing in a mix of languages assisted by the discoveries of books which seems to happen more and more these days. Our clan has been together in the far north of what was previously an area referred to as Scandinavia for just over 40 years. Shelter is mainly the remains of high-rise apartment blocks that were not too badly damaged during the 'event', or indeed the terrible aftermath when those of surviving Man railed as pacts against other surviving Man individuals or groups. This slaughter, through the late 2040s into the early 2050s, once again reflected the inherent need by one or more to dominate any others. As the need to find protection against nuclear fallout contamination became the essential to survive, these episodes soon disappeared.

By the mid-2060s, it was finally realised that long-term survival was possible. Collective groups started working together irrespective of previous race, creed, politics or religious doctrine. All were attempting to build a basic and safe environment in which to live. This was such a small step but was also an awakening at last that by sharing knowledge, experiences or skills, it is possible to create communities offering opportunity for the future without prejudice. So many of these communities were established in the northern sector. By 2080, each clan provided six individuals to be their representatives in the formation of the local community authority.

Some 800 such clans are today represented, having agreed to establish common civil rules and a relationship management programme adopted and used between each clan. Of more importance, however, the building from known technology methods of a constant supply of decontaminated water delivery system to each clan.

Information was shared on potential crop farming methods with each community utilising sites for this purpose within their own area. In addition, and recognising the dangers, some former farm animals such as pigs together with ducks, rabbits and geese were rounded up for examination to assess their potential safe use. However, constant exposure at ground level to the sodden toxic rains of several decades just a few non-contaminated offspring were reared recently at underground pig farms. These have been very successful in providing meat to a number of local clans.

Therefore, a level of shared community drive now exists with all helping to restore some form of comfortable and continual Man life. Interchange of ideas about a vast array of subjects with other communities via radio is now giving opportunity for the Man population here in this northern sector to be optimistic about the years ahead. Every effort is being made to improve on the current infant mortality rate with new anti-contamination medical advances. It is accepted though that this will be a slow process. So much has been lost by the collective actions of those who were here before us. However, there has existed for some time, an underlying cautious-hope for a better future.

Now should have been 2101 in the 22nd century of Man.

(Version 3)

Echoes in a Void

What is truth...?
                    What is life...?
                        What is real?
    Help!   What is war...? What is pain...?

What is love...?
                    What is gain...?
                        What is money...?

What is reason...?
                    What is power...?
                        What is religion...?
    Help!   What is heat...?
    What is shame...?
    What is teaching...?

    Help!
    What is time...?
                    What is yours...?
                        What is mine...?

What is young...?
                    What is old...?
                        What is laughter...?

What is crude…?

Help!   What is cold…?

   What is that…?

     What is crying…?

  What is nude…?

  What is living…?

  What is dying…?

  What is death…?

  What is dead…?

  Help!   What is sleep…?

  What is sorrow…?

  Help!

  Compassion, Hope, Acceptance and Future.

Can This Be True?

Despondency no longer reigns across our lives, watching, waiting, for tomorrow. Optimism is there very deep within, an exciting ever richer stunning tableaux. Here the prospects of a new possibility born from terrible yesteryears has set our hearts afire, our energies aglow. Hope at finally knowing tomorrow holds the key as compassion, each for the other, is now a Man reality. This single acknowledgement changes our view, our understanding of what can be achieved, ensuring that tomorrow's tomorrows provide peace with opportunity for all that Man can be.

Stepping smartly forward into a future where hate no longer reigns supreme, it's replaced with wonder of knowing that together we really can succeed. It isn't stuff that dreams were once made of, nor silent whispers across an autumn breeze. It is with joy we have found the answer of how to share the journey forward in friendship and with ease.

Even when some future challenges are hard, as many are expected to be, we are focused, ready collectively, reaching out towards our proven-feasibility. No longer shall we poison the air, the water or the trees, the insects nor animals, because we fully understand their needs. Our children will be guided to acknowledge any and all other creeds, learning in preparation for when they take on the responsibilities inherent in our deeds.

Nothing now can ever be as it was before because love for a global community actually means so very much more. No one will kill the other but seek only to discover differences, discussing and agreeing that truth shall be the key. Look towards the future, seek out new horizons beyond this earth's sky, in that giant space above your head, it's where your futures lie. Man shall reach to the cosmos together, no matter what personal beliefs are held, seeking peace across the heavens enjoying greater empathy thereby.

RAS (September 2017)

Compassion

Have you ever noticed how the world responds when a substantial natural disaster occurs? An earthquake or massive storm resulting in terrible flooding are but just two examples. Without hesitation, nations and peoples across the world will not wait to hear the cry for help but will offer facilities and support to the Man victims of such an episode. This, despite any political, cultural, religious doctrine and/or often apparent conflicts that may exist between those compassionate nations or people and the affected nation or nations. There are today caring individuals when such a disaster occurs in almost every nation on earth. The power of the reactive, collective compassion for humanity at such incidents totally dwarfs all other differences or Man conflicts. International medical sciences support for children with life-threatening conditions reflects yet another level of collective effort, again even where political or cultural conflict may potentially exist.

No one can doubt then that there resides in virtually all Man a common conscious recognition that human life is precious. It is this recognition that such compassion is in all Man that may yet provide the key to that often desired, meaningful and warm global-handshake. A handshake that has the potential to create opportunity to move humanity forward from its own awful behavioural history of mistrust, fear, anger, frustration, war and hate. The readiness to help and support Man in times of crisis is not driven by hate, but compassion. This is not just something of an imagined silly myth.

The recent Ebola crisis in West Africa is a true example of compassionate humanity offering support teams from around the world assisting in the fight to save lives, irrespective of any dangers to themselves. Together many nations all worked in unison to fight this killer virus. Such is the power of human compassion that race, creed, language or culture or historical differences at these times of Man distress mean absolutely nothing. The recent earthquake in Mexico, together with the devastation across the Caribbean and the southeastern states of USA, in 2017, have resulted in massive support from many countries working with international and local aid organisations.

Compassion has seen millions of refugees fleeing war and/or persecution in their home countries. Here again, the countries who can, and are not any part of the conflict, provide shelter, comfort, water, necessary food, and medical support. Where these displaced peoples are unable to return to their former country, they are, subject to certain conditions, provided with opportunity to remain in the host countries or move to settle in other countries.

Such action clearly confirms that human compassion at the time of conflict or calamity will emerge to support in collective strength to help those affected. However, of even greater magnitude, such help provides for the people surviving these calamities a real **hope** for their tomorrows. Not only is Man to Man compassion expressed on an international level, as indicated above, it is also reflected at national level in many countries across a multitude of issues.

In the UK, for example, there is a yearly 'Children in Need' televised event that consistently raises many tens of millions of pounds from donations by the British public, institutions and businesses. This level of national compassion specifically reflects on the collective desire to help children both locally and internationally, who are and will be, of course, the people of tomorrow. In a way, such compassion is already looking to provide opportunity for a better Man life. As indeed, so many other charities in many countries in and around the world are doing.

Man is able to respond collectively in a positive multicultural way at such times. Recent terrorist attacks, designed to spread fear in some populations across the world, result in the exact opposite reaction. They bring the public together, in unity, support and compassion for those affected directly by each event of this nature. In reality then, acts of terrorism are doomed to failure because they provide the catalyst to heighten the national and international human power of compassion. The more atrocious the event of terrorism the greater is the multicultural collective compassion.

Here again, in such acts, we witness the narcissistic stupidity of Man in its raw inhumaneness. Those who champion such acts of terror, those who condone or build and breed excuses for these atrocities only do so, in my view, for just two reasons. Their desire to manipulate followers (that Man need to control other Man idiot thing) and to garner personal standing in power and wealth, no matter the human cost. The tool used most often by these individuals is that old, trusted friend of Man, propaganda in all its perverse cunning artifice shades. So, where is hope…?

This World of Men

Why do men cheat and lie?
Will it go against them when they die?
Or is it because they want life's best,
Is that why they lie and cheat the rest?
Oh, is money all that is needed in Life?
You damn well know it isn't!
But still you lie to your fellow men,
Just to prove yourself better than them!
Then, when you want something from life
You pander and purr!

I'm sick of the sight of you on your knees.
Why not stand on your own two feet,
Letting the rest of them lie and cheat!

RAS (1966–1968)

Hope

I retain in my memory the following comment I heard in a discussion: *If you continue to hope, you will only be disappointed. So, give up hope, then you'll have nothing to worry about.*

Strictly speaking, where hope is the last defence of a dilemma, Man will indeed worry about the outcome. This may result in an agonising period of disquiet, increased heart rate, and constant fear of disappointment at what may transpire. I suggest, however, that these reactions are nothing to do with hope at all. They are a reflection of insecurity. Man appears to allow the entrance of doubt to acquire an elevation in status not befitting it. Once doubt exists, it often takes charge in the hearts and minds of those with hope. If this is true, we know that hope is definitely opposite to insecurity and doubt.

In its simplest form, the Man sentiment towards hope is an expectation based on aspiration to reach a desired result. It is therefore an optimism or prospect that the outcome will be positive. Simply giving up hope is denying all the real attributes of the word itself. Without hope, Man cannot move towards a better future for our descendants. Without hope we will wallow as individuals, as nations, as Man. With hope, however, we will be able to construct a path towards an inclusive and collective future.

Hope is the fundamental result of the power of human compassion. Time following time, where there has been some awful occurrence, Man-made or not, compassion for those who suffer provides a new hope, from desperation to the development of new opportunities. It is this astonishing ability to create togetherness through compassion and hope that will lead to a new approach to Man behaviour. The 21st century must be the epoch of the awakening of Man to truth, honour and respect for each other. Such a change is not impossible.

However, continuing to be driven by our historical behaviours of greed, or revenge, or in self-interest, the outcome will be catastrophic mayhem. Grasping the power of compassion and generating hope will deliver countless greater beneficial horizons for a positive long-term survival future of our species.

If personal wellbeing, access to water, food and shelter is the need of all Man, why then are there so many poor destitute people without proper access to these life basics in the world today? Millions and millions are living in squalor and daily survival is excruciatingly hard. Where is world compassion? Is it fair to suggest that each of these people may have little or no hope for a better future? Surely, they seek help for themselves, if not, then for their descendants? When they start each day struggling to feed the children, is it fair to say that they will have hope to achieve their objective? Or, is each one driven by pure desperation into the most common of historical Man behaviours, to steal, cheat and lie?

Imagine the possible impact if on one day the depth of compassion that Man displays for those devastated by floods and earthquakes, etc., suddenly arrived on the doorstep of the millions living in abject poverty across the world. Imagine the enormous level of hope that would be generated.

Would this action build a real capacity for hope in a yet unimagined collective future for all Man? Unleashing this power of hope may be the first real collective Man opportunity leading to the very first step in a radical change of collective behaviour. There is no argument to suggest that the world of Man cannot afford to undertake such an expression of compassion. It is absolutely true that Man in the 21st century has the resources, the power, the knowledge and money at its figure-tips to eradicate world poverty. All that is required is the (political) will to do so. (An observation espoused by a former Secretary General of the UN, Mr Kofi Annan.) Or that organising such a complex task would take years of potential political infighting, discussion, compromise and debate.

Such silly arguments occur as to how much money and energy each of the 193 full members of the UN must allocate. Perhaps even including ridiculous discussion such as, if 'our' time and money contributed to this humanitarian effort is less than 'yours' will our country have less political sway or recognition in the outcome? Or, what happens if our country cannot or will not be a part of this process? A million questions or more, all of self-clan-interest. All such questions and debate are stupid in the extreme and will simply show those who want to remain in their own isolation.

The real answer to all such questions is so very easy. Ignore yesterday. The only decision that needs to be made is, does Man of the 21st century recognise the need to change its Man to Man historical behaviours. In agreeing to do so, while at the same lifting millions and millions out of poverty. There can be no reflection of any kind in quantifying what each country has contributed. Neither is there any discussion of or after the event on any political influence on the nations where such a process has been undertaken.

Yes, handing over sufficient knowledge to those nations who have directly benefited from this collective effort will include opportunity to progress with their own governing methodology. Any countries may thereafter offer specific skills and knowledge where the recipient nation requests assistance. The results of such an international cooperation to resolve the hideous status of countless millions will surely generate an avalanche of hope. This will open the recipients' minds to new concepts, new awareness and new challenges that may provide a major redirection for Man-to-Man relationships going forward. Culture changes as a result of greater understanding and knowledge following this process may cause friction but if managed with respect and tolerance, such potential clashes can be overcome and resolved.

This provision and encouragement of hope via the compassionate behaviour of a united and determined humanity will go a very long way towards shaking off the shackles of the past. Perhaps resulting in the discovery of many new probabilities in securing a safe journey forward for all mankind.

All this can be and is definitely possible without encroaching on the culture, language, religious beliefs or sovereignty of any nation. By creating hope together, Man may at last be able to banish its own ghosts of the past forever, leading to a whole new giant relationship leap forward for mankind.

Renewable Life

The continued production and use of the industrialisation period necessities such as oil, coal and gas, iron ore and steel, together with many nasty others which are direct derivatives of the aforementioned, has placed much of Mother Nature's living species in serious jeopardy. This reality, alongside the very cast-off and throw-away behaviour characteristics of Man, demands urgent repair and attention.

It is already understood that something as simple as 'plastic' is dumped across the world by Man at the rate of many millions of tonnes per year. This is set to become the second Man-made largest threat to its own continued survival on this planet. Clearly the first is, of course, Man itself. Recent reports on current and future ocean pollution levels suggest that potentially there will be more cast-aside plastic objects in the oceans of the world than fish by the year 2050. We have already seen that without water, Man cannot survive. With oceans polluted with plastics, nuclear and human waste, not only will marine life be potentially destroyed but the rain-cycle providing fresh water on land will be severely compromised.

The potential is that acid-rain will reach a state of worldwide harm levels way beyond anything that Man can cure or control. The level of that vital miniscule world organism, Plankton, will reduce significantly and without a collective action taken now, will most definitely signal that our time on earth is over. Renewable 'clean' energy is the current flavour of the century. However, this cannot be developed in isolation and must be just one part of a much wider project, that of *Renewable Life*. Here again is a project that cannot succeed without hope.

It is now time to ensure that knowledge and technology is used to develop a planet wide *renewable life* capability. The application of the power of collective hope may become the only way to address the current appalling pollution dangers that all species on our planet face. The development of renewable energy capabilities is only the beginning of attempting to secure clean energy needs. These renewables cannot just be for the benefit of the so-called 'developed' nations of the world. The idiocy of undertaking such a development by and for just a small seemingly privileged group of Man collectives will only succeed in creating an even wider gap between the haves and the have-nots on a global basis.

The development of renewable energy resources, therefore, must result in the worldwide application of both the knowledge and the methodology simultaneously. Failure of the developed countries to do so will ostracise large sections of humanity while at the same time diminish substantially any potential 'clean air' benefits due to the vagaries of the world's weather patterns.

The concept of *renewable life* is that of again changing behaviour. Whereas Man has 'progressed' in the past by utilising natural resources for its own particular gain, this was often in ignorance of any possible dangers to any other species. Renewable energy development should be only one part of the overall process for ensuring *renewable life* for all Mother Nature's living species.

There are so many individuals and organisations expressing concerns about the current level of Man pollution across the world in these early years of the 21st century. Research projects into alternative waste disposal methods that do not damage the planet are ongoing. Here, then, is another important step towards the development of *renewable life*. Remembering that the world population of Man is expected to grow to 11 billion by the year 2101 this level of Man population growth will ensure that the consumption of the earth's remaining survival resources will shrink drastically. Without a worldwide drive to effectively support such a huge population growth by collectively designing a fully encompassing *renewable life* process, any stand-alone renewable energy system will falter. A much wider programme for the benefit of all species on earth has to be established.

Perhaps this one overall project will at last result in all members of the UN actively participating in, and working in line with the word and intent expressed in the UN charter to which they have all agreed to. The collective power of hope generated by compassion will, over time, erode the negative habits of millions of years of Man. Race, creed, wealth, power and knowledge standing side by side for the first time to collectively plan a shared future for humanity. This will ensure that constant development and achievements of each new generation following on from the last can recognise the right of all Man societies to live in peace irrespective of whatever their doctrine, religion or political structure is. Grasp the simple truth that no single human is born to hate, or kill, any other. Rather, each within their own society may learn to participate in a productive contribution both to their own society and where desired, to any or all other Man societies in the world.

Open, non-propaganda-twisted education leading to understanding and knowledge will ensure continued emergence of new hope, ideas and concepts on all manner of Man activities and behaviours. These then can be shared with all humanity and the outcome will not be that I, we, are better than any other or others. Open dialogue and discussion in all survival matters will flourish.

Here then, in the collective development of a *renewable life* programme, perhaps the dominant target together could contain the flexibility for the creation of unimaginable Man development progress for the next millennium and more. All as a result of harnessing the power of compassion and the resultant hope.

Acceptance

Individually, we may be weak, fragile, often self-centred and afraid. Once 'comfortable' in our own surroundings, we try to protect our world from the pretentious and the so-called fake or propaganda of others. Even though, 'our way' will indeed encompass both these falsifications. Well, that is how we all mostly perceive others. The exceptions to this are very rare indeed and only happen when we can see personal advantage. Such a capacity is a constant companion of us all, although, until reaching the state of recognised independent adult it will be governed and controlled, for the most part, by our parents and clan culture.

Nevertheless, our individual own characteristics nurtured as a child provide the background of who we interact, react and accept into our own personal world. It could be suggested that we have a choice in who we get close to. For example, the similarities there may be perceived by us in others background which could result in sharing a positive relationship or not. So very often, and without really recognising it, the majority of Man will only develop caring relationships with those similar to 'our own' disposition and circumstances. In other words, it is basically easier and more comfortable to get along with and accept our culturally 'close equivalent' Man. Acceptance of others, their colour, background, language, religion or political diversity will all cause hesitation, perhaps even a backing-off or possible refusal to share space and time with such other Man due to imagined difficulty in diverse ideologies.

Acceptance of and even into others' cultures will require that as a first step we must, at a national and individual level, peel away all the propaganda driven areas of acceptance behaviour that reflect the culture of our own kin, clan or tribe. For example, that we are the best, that our clan and cultural rules or religion are 'better' than any others. Without such an approach we will not succeed in building an internationally recognised honest relationship behaviour. It is the historic behaviour of almost enforcement that cannot be inflicted by us on those in a culture we look to understand.

Similarly, we must not reflect any abhorrence of, or to, any activities prevalent in others' society behaviour. The approach process has to be a willingness to learn of such matters while at the same time welcoming others without fear to learn of our culture and behaviours. The building of a real or metaphorical wall to keep citizens land-locked into the society into which they have been born, is still in existence across this planet of ours even today.

Learning the reasoning behind such an inward-facing society in the 21st century is essential. To be successful, acceptance will only be possible when we all allow all citizens to learn of other nations' cultures, learnings, structures and future potential opportunities.

Yes, some nations, creeds or clans will continue to deny openness and to ignore genuine requests to share their lifestyles with others. However, reluctance of a few to participate in true openness must not derail the journey of all. Rather, they must be seen simply as attitudes driven by their own historical circumstances that lead to reticence. It will require a strong collectiveness of responsibility in generating a common approach by so many differing cultures to establish and share in a positive working environment. An environment in which they can all participate for the development of a long-term secure future. A future *renewable life* capability. This, by building the history of tomorrow, today. The reticent will notice progress and opportunity to learn. They must know that participation is always open and that they are welcome to contribute.

It is as true today as it has always been that the action of war, in reality, is as a result of not accepting, or stubbornly even, never really attempting to explore any common ground opportunities that may exist to resolve an imagined national or international conflict. The processes and environment of the UN which was 132stablishhed in 1945 as a conflict resolution provider clearly has so often failed and continues to do so today. In other words, the fundamental principles are and remain broken.

An urgent review of the capacity of a single permanent member nation of the UN Security Council to veto' any action taken on a UN Security Council resolution, must be undertaken. It is astounding that once the majority have approved or agreed a resolution that just 1 nation state can prevent the implementation of that resolution. The 21st century world is so very more complex and challenging than that of 1945. Here is why the UN is broken.

China, France, Russia, the United Kingdom and the United States of America are the five nations with permanent member status of the Security Council. A title awarded to each of these nations who were collectively seen as 'victors' of the second world war. Clearly the true concept of the democratic process is omitted with this august collection of nations with such a power. Here again we see an elite exclusive environment of national protectionism embedded in the so-called United Nations for the benefit and use of just 5 nations of the 193 members. Without change, such a capability will forever see national self-interest of each of these nation as a constant and possibly acting as a corrupt annihilation of the very clear essence and intention of the UN charter.

Acceptance can also be denied due to the extreme depth of academic and or technical complexities of any society. Put another way, the 'keep-it-simple-stupid', attitude period in the mid to late 20th century may actually have contained some real hidden wisdom. Where societies, mainly in the developed world, have romped ahead in the development of science in multitudes of technologies in communications, computerisation, transportation and medical fields, two potentially very destructive issues have emerged.

First, the more complex a process is, the more difficult it is to understand, repair, alter or amend. The result of such complexity, over time, will be that less and less individual Man will hold complete knowledge of the entire process itself. The second issue, which is directly due to the first, is what happens should the process ever fail? Recovery, if needed, may prove to be increasingly more and more difficult and time consuming. Man, reliance on the process itself may be almost absolute.

Such a complex process, where multiple amendments and improvements have been made, will then raise a question as to the real benefits of the process itself. In other words, the most complex threat to any such process is Man itself. The constant human clash of intelligent process is driven by those without knowledge.

A recent example of this, and perhaps a timely warning can be seen with the sudden total collapse of the entire computer system utilised by one of the largest and leading world airlines. The crash caused tens of thousands of passengers to be stranded across the world, thousands of flights cancelled and general havoc across all the services of the affected airline and many others, not to mention the horror of the knock-on effect across airports and airlines around the planet. This took very many days to recover from, cost the airline huge amounts of compensation and reputational damage!

After investigation, the airline announce that it had been caused by 'Human Error'. Without a comprehensive acceptance that such processes may demand full international cooperation in monitoring, testing, disaster-recovery planning and improvements, the potential of a system failure could prove true and possibly catastrophic. Acceptance must be in sharing of resources, of intellectual capacity and in particular, knowledge, to correct or repair any such failure. Comprehensive Man to Man acceptance of differences will prove to be an inspirational step into the world of tomorrow leading to greater avoidance of incidents such as the airline issue above. Acceptance that the continuance of historic Man to Man behaviour cannot provide a future for this planet and all its living species is the only real future path to follow.

Change is difficult, challenging and often so full of potential to fail. However, if we truly want our children's great-grandchildren to be a reality, Man of today cannot fail. We each arrived naked, innocent, the only certainty for all of us is that there is an end to each of us. It is the difference we can each make in our short time here that is the foundation for tomorrow's future of all species sharing life on this world.

Acceptance

I am me and you are you, together we share so many similarities,
You were born, so was I, each helpless and reliant on our relatives.
I am 'black', you perhaps 'white', 'brown' or 'yellow' or even a mix.
You may be female, I am male, yet we share no knowledge of this,
I am sure we may cry a lot looking for food, for attention or a kiss.
In newborn innocence, we had an open canvas on which to paint,
In truth, it was used by life all around us to learn and concentrate.

I now speak and read a language, so very different from your own,
I am taught very differently perhaps from where you have a home.
I am now an adult all innocence corrupted in the way I think of you,

I am incessantly told we are of the best, in all we believe, say or do.
I am singing rousing songs attesting to apparent glories of our past,
I am now aware of amended facts so I know some real truth at last.
I will not accept adjusted cultural twists in this I am really steadfast.

Neither you nor I were ever born to kill despise, spurn, loathe or hate,
These are things that we are taught, reflecting our cultures mandate.
We must reach across these false barriers, across such a social divide,
I will travel to meet with you without fear or an engineered clan pride.
Will you and I both stand in peace, listening, exploring our future fate?
Working together in sharing knowledge, openly learning, without hate,
Taking a daring new human step into a hope for all man to participate.

Having worked together, side by side, giving each support for the truth,
Helping all other communities to advance in sharing a brand-new oath.
When our time here is over, and we move forward into the next realm,

We will stand together in awe of those who take our place at the helm.

Thank you for your knowledge, sharing your clans' culture, so candidly,

Tomorrow now is set to be a world full of peace that we shall never see.

But together, we know, and we are assured, of an everlasting harmony.

RAS (November 2017)

Is This the Way to Tomorrow?

That the hope arising in every current resident across multiple dialogues will produce astounding Man awakening rewards. Open cultural concept exchanges, each Man collective sharing basic clarity of purpose of own Clan, Kin and Nation in full naked truth without frosted untrue colourings.

Compassion and hope for continued Man existence driving away future uncertainty. Acceptance that cultures are indeed different but that each and all have the right to life. Building a safe tomorrow without poverty, war, ignorance and fear can create a global human oneness. The ability, time and application to explore collectively with open recognition of and for all of Earth's species survival rights and needs. Each can publicly give, without revile, recognition of constant simple truths now laid bare that:

Weapons do not mass-kill people. People mass-kill people.

Plastics kill nature, human waste and conceit kills clean air, land and oceans. Deforestation destroys all-natural plant life, insects and countless land and marine life forms that until the advent of modern Man were living in shared harmony. Wealthy and egocentric, mercenary Man has absolutely no future power.

Human compassion, hope, knowledge and truth are the only powers for the long-term survival of all living things on our planet.

On January 2018: ALL LIVING THINGS ON OUR PLANET NOW RELY ON MAN FOR CONTINUED SURVIVAL.

It is now time to pull together and design a tomorrow with and for those of tomorrow, that will safeguard all future tomorrows. Demand for change is already arising from the populace masses who, through education, knowledge and understanding, know that the past Man-deeds of destruction, savagery, greed and subsequent denial cannot exist in the world of tomorrow. This is not a riotous unruly act of disobedience, nor a seeking for, or demanding of, retribution, but a simple common stance that the continuance of Man behaviours of yesterday can only ensure that this planet will soon be devoid of all current existing life forms.

Are you ready to help clean the air of tomorrow?

Can you foresee a new dawn for all life forms of tomorrow?

Will you take hold of the hand of all humanity seeking out that new dawn of tomorrow?

All to ensure that those of tomorrow, whom we shall not see, have their own tomorrows?

Fear of the unknown is a false malaise that may cause hesitation in stepping onto and along a new path. Reluctance to move forward together may prevail. Those without fear, though, by taking the lead and stepping forward, will ensure that a possible new Man future reality can be achieved. While fear counsels caution, this in itself looks to drive for more information, understanding and therefore potentially an opportunity to expand knowledge further. Knowledge will provide the strongest support, but by far the broadest positive impact for, and on, Man will be that driven by a collective hope.

So many differing future scenarios can be explored though a united Man community, that the options will be endless. A simple recognition that mass Man employment opportunity as experienced in and during the industrialised period will soon not be an option due to robotics and computerisation of most mass production lines. The future of education itself is now open to a wide and never-ending number of change-opportunities to meet the skills anticipated being necessary to support all potential new endeavours.

Such is the huge array of specialist needs and social demands to meet the future that the very process of education and sharing of knowledge itself will demand employment of a continuous rethink programme. Of course, sciences of every description and some yet to be discovered will most definitely require multiple skill levels, the complexities of which will be far reaching. The same will apply to engineering, medical and social support education.

Spreading cultural awareness will see opportunity for gaining understanding and knowledge of traditions and behaviours. Experts in all spoken languages must also sit alongside experts of all electronic languages. Here again exists more opportunity for the development of future education programmes. There is no limit to the exploration or beneficial progress both for all Man and the natural world in which we currently reside.

AI (Artificial Intelligence?)

Reference to 'Artificial Intelligence' in the second half of the 20th century and early 21st century is often depicted in news programmes and industry magazines. Robotics to medical sciences, engineering to space exploration will occupy news headlines with insights and extraordinary statements of exciting Man opportunities to create, repair and potentially eradicate many life-threatening diseases. However, it just as regularly disappears from public view into silence, often for quite a long time! It does appear, though, to live in the minds of many as perhaps the ultimate, even maybe the panacea, for all future Man opportunities and woes. Let's take a moment now to undertake a simple exploration into what 'AI' may really be. Starting with a look at the English definitions of each word.

Artificial: *False, Fake, Contrived, Imitation, Feigned, Pretend, Insincere, Synthetic and Man-Made!*

Intelligence: *Intellect, Acumen, Aptitude, Astuteness, Clever, Gifted, logical, Perceptive not Man-Made!*

A comment I heard many years ago when someone made reference to the development of AI was that, "There is no such thing as AI. Something either is or isn't intelligent."

Of course, Man is currently looking to such things as 'driverless' modes of transport, including rail and road traffic, aircraft and perhaps in the not too distant future, spacecraft. All the above can and will be achieved but they are physical machines and cannot be 'intelligent'. They will be the result of Man's Intelligence capabilities, application and design abilities. This will apply to all matters of an evolving technological nature. But no one can deny that, even with the greatest strides in knowledge so far, Man remains fallible.

Despite intricate and complex tasks of, and for, outstanding benefits, errors have been made. Disasters do happen, often with very tragic results. The truly magnificent issue, though, that has been proven time and time again, is that Man can and does *learn* from such mistakes. It is this single ability to interrogate, learn, argue, amend, rebuild and resolve the errors that reflects a unique intellect that resides in Man. This places Man in the top position of intelligence of all Mother Nature's issue, although that argument itself has yet to be proven!

Driverless transport vehicles are but one step towards building a 'machine' that incorporates Man's knowledge levels. These machines will be filled with such knowledge of computerisation, satellite communication, ground-positioning, all-round smart visual proximity, road rules, instant communications and monitoring technologies that while performing its allotted functionality the future Man occupants will have little or even no idea, or even want to know, 'how-it-all-works'!

Examples of this are easy to find. Ask your friend or family member how a phone or television actually works. Unless they are somehow directly involved in these areas, they are most likely to reply "I don't know how either work, but do I need to know?" Such future transport 'machines' will not, of their own accord, have capacity to *learn*, think or argue. Only when something built by Man is capable of real self-learning, thinking and reasoning, correcting and improving and reproducing itself without Man, can these activities potentially be regarded as the use of non-Man-made intelligence. At which point and with such a capability, this also then cannot truly be called *Artificial* intelligence.

I submit, therefore that when Man applies all its immense knowledge to the building of driverless transports, it is nothing more than recognising its own power of knowledge and ability to do so. AI (Artificial Intelligence) as currently advocated, in reality, cannot ever exist. Many fellow species on our planet do show a level of intelligence in their own species survival, but no other species has yet reached the same magnificence of intellect prowess as Man.

All other species on this planet have placed their very continuous existence of life in the hands of Man! Only a collective sharing knowledge openly towards an agreed solution has any chance of securing a long-term 'life' future on Earth. Are we perhaps destroying the origin of Man?

The Origin of You and Me

Here is that draw of the shining sea, so blue,
Building a passion of quiet in me, oh so true.
Here is our origin, deep within the sea of joy
For all to arise from slumber and shout ahoy!

No raging waves nor sharp eruptions of hate
Simply an invite to share and to participate.
Washing away anger, offering peace sublime
Pausing to cast asunder fear for Humankind.

The peace that the calm blue waters can bring
Rendering no harm but a pleasant quiet within.
So small and fragile are we standing by the sea
Here flow the waters, the origin of you and me.

A serene sense of wonder holds me by the sea
Guiding me to stop rushing to value tranquillity.
No matter what or where the future lies for thee
Here flow the waters, the origin of you and me.

RAS (2017)

The Falsehood of Money

Money, a commodity that is chased after, fought over, exchanged, robbed, stolen and saved. Used constantly as the basis of all corruption within the relentless wealth hunt across the world of Man. But, despite constant demand, there never seems to ever be enough to go around. The community of Man, both individually and collectively, across the world are always seeking more. But while some continuously gain a hold on this 'money stuff', the vast majority continuously struggle to gain any, some, have none at all.

Which is really odd considering that basically it only has to be printed by a machine somewhere, which can happen at the press of a button! (*The very same way the next war can happen—at the press of a button!*) So, why the constant chase for this commodity? Is this possibly yet another propaganda trick to keep the masses insecure and in their allotted place towards the bottom of the Man heap? It cannot be too difficult to grasp that the reality of this stuff called money is that its 'value' is an imagined or nebulous feeling or expectation at any one moment in time. Its 'value' is an invisible fluctuation of perceived worth controlled within a secret shadowy society in each nation's elite? It has, however, if sufficient money is acquired, the capacity to purchase things which then become 'owned' perhaps also becoming assets of an individual Man or Man collective or nation.

The acquisition of money is derived from uncountable Man activities, some via socially and morally acceptable activities and just as much, possibly more, is generated via non-socially acceptable and immoral activities. Measurement of wealth of an individual, business enterprise or country is calculated at a simple level in the following way 'assets less liabilities = wealth'. It is having this 'money stuff' that enables the acquisition of wealth.

When looking at wealth on a global basis, the astonishing thing is that in 2017, 85% of world-wealth was owned by just 10% of the wealthiest Man population of the world. The remaining 90% of adults hold just 15% of the world's wealth between them. The world estimated total wealth in 2017, is in the region of US$280+Trillion. There are many well respected organisations who undertake research and constantly monitor such statistics and provide information on the internet to enable interested parties to view their findings.

So, the 'Falsehood' is that money itself has no actual 'value' whatsoever. It is just 'stuff' with which it is possible to purchase or acquire things. The item or items acquired may only be of 'value' to that purchaser. A loaf of bread, for example, purchased by a very poor person may be seen to hold great 'value' as a life-saving acquisition for self or kin. That same loaf, purchased by a more fortunate individual will simply be regarded as part of a family or kin dietary everyday food with no thought of 'value' at all. It is therefore the ownership of a thing or things that this money 'stuff' is used for.

It offers the ability to purchase something that is of 'value', therefore there is no actual 'value' in money itself. Yet the entire world of Man is driven by the desire for money and the resultant wealth it may provide.

Such idiocy in collective Man behaviour has contributed to the multiple chasms of destruction proliferated over the aeons of time by and between Man.

Real Man Value

Real Man value is not reliant on money stuff at all because it is always there, inside each of us. Even if we ignore it and hide it away deep within our clan, kin, society behaviour rules. The value we each have is never too far beyond our reach. An individual's primary essence must surely be for compassion towards others, irrespective of how we are each perceived. Where there are eyes shining in love or laughter, or arms holding a new born baby, even standing among fields of flowers, the anticipation of joy and of hope for the future always resides within.

Value is in sharing the joys of the many languages and beliefs and collectively understanding that we are all a single microscopic miracle born of one magnificent world around us and beneath our feet. Learning and laughing, sharing time and knowledge, building a true trust are values that are for everyone. No need for money at all here. These non-money Man traits together in the current climate of significant change hold the future, if there is to be one, and, therefore, will prove to be of far more value and power especially when aligned with Man collective hope and acceptance.

Among the old establishment, the wealthy and purchased elite, there is in this second decade of the 21st century a growing disquiet, an agony in a large portion of this particular Man population irrespective of location, nationality or doctrine. It is especially severe in those whose families of yesteryear or yester-centuries obtained their status and wealth from pillaging, slave trading, slaughtering and purloining across multiple lands and enforcement control of enslaved colonies.

Their current dilemma is the conscious detection in their ranks that the spoils of war, mass Man degradation and administered ignorance, all of which helped to create and keep their high wealth status, are no longer in abundance. They are also acknowledging that their imparting false walls of propaganda and deception have collapsed beyond any possible repair and can no longer be utilised. Their historical role is over, gone, abolished. Emerging out of many centuries of subservient state the mass educated populations of the developed countries are demanding truth through the acquisition of knowledge, international populace relationship building and unrestricted awareness of social and civil differences.

It is this drive that is capable of offering plentiful new concepts, ideas and answers to building a future Man-world of inclusion, protection, opportunity and fairness. All this reflects the urge to apply real value that has little or no relationship with the 'money stuff'. Of course, 'money stuff' may continue to be used as the tool to acquire life products and services but isn't it time that money stuff was of equal purchase ability anywhere across the planet?

Currently, a single article of value purchased—a loaf of bread—in one country costing two bits of 'money stuff' may require the exchange of 5 bits of 'money stuff' in another country. This discrepancy in purchase value, where the commodity is, essentially the same, is reflective of the perceived worth of that country's 'money stuff' measured against that country's perceived economic status somehow related to a nation's gold bullion holdings verses its level of debt. Assets/minus Liabilities/equals Wealth. With just one type of 'money stuff' across the world, the mystique and associated mistrust by the populace generally will drive towards a more globally and publicly acceptable methodology of a true and reflective international benchmark for the measurement of purchase value.

This would mean that it looks the same and represents an equality between all nations. Not something that is surrounded by a mythical, nonsense behaviour of spectral secrecy by each country. In the past, something called a 'Gold Exchange Standard' has been the basis on which a 'fixed value' is placed on a piece or pieces of 'money stuff' by a government guaranteeing an exchange rate to another country that also uses the gold exchange standard irrespective of what type of local 'money stuff' is used as a means of the exchange.

The same could apply to a single piece of world 'money stuff' taking away the nebulous conflict between any national perception and a worldwide currency. Knowledge, via education and shared experience, honesty and openness, is of far more power in the 21st century than this 'money stuff' can ever be. ***Money cannot buy the future of our planet*** or indeed of the human species.

It can, however, efficiently take all living things into the oblivion that is potentially a state of *echoes in the void* or a non-Man-tomorrow. The only way to avoid such a situation is by all Man working together, in a fixed and agreed way to secure a collective behaviour change for the future benefit of us all.

There is no choice here. There cannot be anything other than compassion and resultant hope to drive the long-term survival of Man and all other species on this planet. Money and wealth are unable to secure any future for this world.

Holding Hands

Take my hand and lead me to the future you, newly found friends of mine. Together let us seek knowledge that will ensure all life continues forward far beyond our time. A future where love for each will be solidly enshrined. No hate or false jealousy but recognition, no matter the language colour or creed, working as one, with much less haste but a combined and powerful speed. Creating a world of tranquillity, of honour, of hope, a world that will provide for all future generations' needs. Cast aside the isolation, greed and cruelty of the past, banishing indifference and all contempt, sharing a common direction together, side by side, solid and steadfast.

Take the theoretical hand of a phantom future child in our collective head to imagine their world full of life, ample nourishment and safe freedoms to explore, no hatred or dread. We shall design a world where the atmosphere is clear, the oceans clean and shining blue. With all Man enjoying a meaningful participation in a shared world, built with passion for life anew. As they explore the universe with a technology, we cannot yet imagine nor even vaguely see, they look to explore the dawn of their own new tomorrows now armed with new knowledge and ability. We cannot progress forward from here nor shall they come back in time to see, that we are all just people, yes, just you and me.

Our role now is done with tomorrow's challenges resolved by us and then won. Changing our behaviour rules to cooperation between each has enabled us to meet tomorrow's future head on. Holding hands in unison not looking to the past, building for tomorrow's children we have climbed through that broken looking-glass. Thank you for taking hold of my hand to guide me on my way. Without your tolerance of me and mine we could have all easily gone astray. I accept that we will really never truly know what success we have achieved but due to our trust in each other the foundation was conceived. Now finally we pass on to those who follow on behind, a future where truth and tolerance stand together, side by side.

RAS (March 2018)

Footnotes/Recent Thoughts

Military spending, 2017: those same 15 countries who were spending some 50% of the world's total spend increased by some 30% to US$1,350 Trillion, for the year ending 2017.

For the year ending 2018, total world spend was US$1,833 trillion of which those same 15 countries accounted for US$1,377 trillion. Why?

Global tree cover loss had risen substantially by the end of 2016 to some 29.7 million hectares—an astonishing 51% increase over the previous year. This is approximately equal to about a land area the size of New Zealand. This huge tree loss was mostly caused by Man-made fires and commercial deforestation for farming expansion, very few from natural events. Currently, in 2019, an area the size of a football pitch is cleared **every single minute of every day** in the Amazon rainforest!

2018 global deforestation reports show a continued massive growth of natural woodlands with replanting recorded at its lowest level ever.

The civil war in Syria continues albeit less favourable in international newsy interest. Only a few IS fighters remain and even less anti-government forces survive but the collection of external political powers remains a constant fight with little or even no attempt at resolution—so the innocent still die!

11 November 2018, 11 am

So, they are to be remembered! Yes, those who died in duty of a fractured, divided royal household! Never mind the level of sacrifice, of loss, of pain and blindness, missing ears, eyes and limbs all gone. Hiding of the reasons in the confused mire with lies and propaganda driving them all not to grow old.

And still we weep

No matter the side or the lines that separated the cheated bamboozled foe their flags lying asunder! They shall be remembered! But the cover-up and immorality of their orchestrated demise is hidden. Those of the privy community, 'the realms', live with the possibility of exposure to a blatant blunder.

And still we weep

New killing machines on the ground, or waters, in the sky, produced to ensure many more will die! War to support the embittered elite families of all languages in discharging their aligned grievances. "We are the affronted," they shout! Thus, their minions take the pre-set rule obeying the battle cry.

And still we weep

What justice has never been wrought upon those whose long-held foibles were the very, real cause! They are the monsters! Their inflated annoyance at each-others behaviour drove the charge to war. These were the sponsors calling the first shots, who will die and who will not, gesticulating no pause.

And still we weep

One hundred years from the chosen end date at 11 am, to some it came just a few moments too late! We shall fall silent for a little space today, offering our respect and to pray for all those many fallen. Never again shall the minions blindly heed the cry of those with injured family pride shouting hate!

And still we weep

The end of the empires! Those false deceitful self-grabbing kings, queens, empires and thiefdoms! Alliances of greed and monstrous political self-entitlement shall now record their own bitter truth. With bowed heads, they stand side by side, seeking to heal the generations of wounds and sorrows.

So, shall we weep?

RAS (this Sunday morning)

Seeing!

Understanding all around us requires perseverance and the urge to see yet often we are blinded, lost in habits of our life slumbers, you and me. We notice not the whole picture, just what is expected and comfortable ignoring actual reality in such behaviour reflecting society rules, affable. Fear of broken dogma forbids us to investigate further than our eyes see hiding from us all they can, not allowing us to absorb to see true reality. Looking without seeing scared to look around so judging where we tread this way, we follow the rules towards a pre-determined, safe path ahead.

Protection from potentials for any alternative view, we lose the true way reaching towards tomorrow's view, trudging along the communities' day. What is normally just commonly accepted without challenge of any fault brings anticipated calm. But open your eyes, to acknowledge the default.

The world of our own society cover-up by many harsh, concocted, truths wraps around each one of us walking along the path of deceits, uncouth. This is covered up deviously, in chartered teachings to children at school the lies amassed over centuries, are attempting order and protecting all. Applaud those following the induced line, chastise all who seek out truth its why we only see what we are taught to see so now we must be sleuth.

Cast aside the foggy shield, stop! Look without time pressure nor anxiety, the truth is there for all to see so drop the phony imposed sham of piety. You can now really learn and appreciate our world in all its humble glory See the real topics of the day in full display; pursue the facts not the story. Only then can we collectively abandon wicked falseness to release us all from our murky past, to hold hands with other cultures by standing tall.

RAS (January 2019)

Fallen Democracy

The dreams of those of yesteryear to take community control of life's events are slipping and sliding now towards an almost invisible mockery or pretence. Our government of and for all the people was that dream's principle premise today we see that one-party rules even lacking full power creating a menace. The referendum question, leave or stay, answered by most, let's move away; two and a half years of verbal conflict is passed without a resolution even today.

Eligible voters participated along democracy lines, the count recorded in full in saying 'leave' so a very clear answer was achieved, but to some, so sorrowful. The party clinging to power by a billion-pound bribe to the small DUP mouse denied any part in negotiations for all the other elected parties of the house. Thus, the fabric for full confrontation across the floor was solidly established every party often quarrelling within itself, some with members so dumfounded.

A century since universal suffrage provided entitlement for all to vote at last members shout for their own version of what to do, the outcome, is a farce. The Great British empire, once a leader in this world, is now seen, as a laugh. European leaders amazed or aghast at former privy-minister's, now outcasts yet still our leaders hold on to the hope that all is not yet lost there is a deal awaiting to be approved by a majority of the house now the trepidations are real.

Let's call another referendum, say some members, but this will raise a debate about the future of democracy, the people's decision is made so it's too late. Now, all the opposition ranks are fearful and look to their party leaders reply to compromise, seek out an acceptable resolution and save democracy, just try! The people's dream, awarded so long ago, must never be destroyed by pride because our children will forever lament this time when our democracy died!

RAS (February 2019)

What Am I Today?

I cannot find a way to justify my stay within this precious place
No more rushing anywhere trying to contribute with any haste
So much knowledge I have in understanding and working hard
No longer needed to help or to participate I can now disregard
It isn't true all the old are resting or unwinding with little to do
I'm now participating in sport writing thoughts and singing too
Many of those working state that we deserve a quiet warm day
Exploring all possibilities our remaining future may have in play

Around the long hours twixt day until night self-indulgence lies
To do all the little silly things as if such is now our compromise
But we cannot engage one's consciousness anywhere to its full
Time of deliberation on what next and not on what is wasteful

Very rare are possibilities to apply skills not many can be found
So, clarity of thought or testing ponderous concepts do abound
Augmenting all those many preposterous concepts in our mind
Still the mystery of our place in this universe is possible to find

Here is the arena in which to play for all those who cannot rest
Seek answers to secure a safe future for all children that is best
Never mind those doubters shouting such cannot ever be done
Show them and the whole world that matters can be overcome
This just requires proper thought and investigations taking time
Seek the challenge in this task knowing answers are rare to find
Opportunity must be found to initiate a better human life style
With all ideas explored their futures are in your hands this while

RAS (April 2019)

I Cannot Cry

There is nothing that will ever be of reward by man to man
slaughter
No privileges no tribute for this behaviour just shame and
dishonour
Yet across our human domain's words of depravity twist
many souls
Blinding them to any reality forcing them to scream without
controls
These are corrupted by those many warped leaders' potent
thoughts
Who are debased by twisted teaching to get revenge so it is
wrought
Such cowardly leaders will never carry out their false
instructed tasks
But shy away to claim innocence behind biased perverted face
masks

Until this vile truth is exposed for all it is to hear and see I
shall not cry
But for the victims' families who have lost eternally all who
had to die

Their sacrifice is a gift to us of the proof that false hate and lies are real
No God or idol of any honour agrees to such acts but only seeks to heal
The 50 slaughtered in New Zealand the other day by bigotry intolerance
Reflects how we must awake to end the bitter lies giving truth a chance
Until exposures of religious hate-teachings is confirmed and so negated
The weak shall be empowered by twisted lies designed to foster hatred

I cannot cry false tears giving the perpetrators chance to sing and smile
As this shall relinquish my soul into their contorted joy, so very infantile
They are not leaders of any human call for peace nor any understanding
Their drive is own status, gratification a warped essence of self-polluting
Power it is that exhausts their own truth so extinguishing their humanity
A leader of themselves no messages of soft tolerance just worship vanity
Never mind the doctrine they hide within or the colour of their own skin
It is they who are degraded secretly encouraged to be so they are the **sin**.

RAS (March 2019)

Here in 2023

Four years further on, during which time simply nothing has changed. No matter all the dreams and hopes of millions of humans across our planet.

Huge increase in military activity country vs country. The loss of hundreds of thousands of lives while Russia invades Ukraine. So many military engagements across this now boiling planet. Every living earth creature, plant is dying. Thus, without a 'Man to Man' agreement to amend our stupidity and attempt to stop the now only and obvious outcome of our failings…Goodbye to all that once was or once could have been.

RAS